THE PAROCHIAL CHAPELRY
OF SADDLEWORTH

A HISTORY AND DESCRIPTION OF THE PAROCHIAL CHAPELRY OF SADDLEWORTH IN THE COUNTY OF YORK

BY JAMES BUTTERWORTH

A FACSIMILE EDITION WITH NEW INTRODUCTION BY ROBERT POOLE

SADDLEWORTH HISTORICAL SOCIETY
UPPERMILL
2006

This edition published 2006
by Saddleworth Historical Society
Saddleworth, Yorkshire, England
www.saddleworth-historical-society.org.uk

The copyright of the Introduction
rests with the author

ISBN 0 904 982 09 2

Printed on cream matt paper
Typeset in Monotype Scotch Roman

Printed and bound by
Smith Settle Printing and Bookbinding Ltd
Ilkley Road, Otley, West Yorkshire, LS21 3JP

List of subscribers to the 2006 edition
r. indicates retired.

Alcock, Denis, Delph, *r.*

Ashton, Wilfred, Great Chesterford, Essex, *r.*

Bardsley, Roy, Uppermill, *r.*

Barnes, John, Diggle, architect.

Barrell, Amy, Woolroad, *r.*

Barrow, Freya, Didsbury, Lancs. customer service agent.

Barrrow, Neil, Carr, chartered management accountant.

Barrow, Tom, Didsbury, Lancs. tv researcher.

Baylis, Linda, Whitby, New Zealand.

Beattie, Enid, Harrop Court.

Beattie, Iain, Harrop Court, optician.

Benson, Oliver, Uppermill, caretaker.

Bogdanovic, Anne, Exeter, Devon, nurse *r.*

Boocock, Frank, Lydgate, teacher *r.*

Boote, George, Carshalton, Surrey, musician.

Billing, Michael, Old Tame, civil servant & yeoman.

Blower, Roy, Grasscroft, *r.*

Blyth, Roderick, Shaw, Lancs. engineer.

Bradbury, David, York, Yorks. librarian.

Bradbury, Peter, Spurstow, Ches. woollen manufacturer *r.*

Bradbury, Sam, Uppermill, sheep farmer.

Broadbent, Albert, Beckermet, Cumb. electrical engineer *r.*

Broadbent, Elsie, Back o' th' Low, membership secretary.

Broadbent, Stanley, Back o' th' Low, chartered engineer *r.*

Buckley, Mike, Dobcross, borough councillor.

Cain, Gail, Hay-on Wye, Brecknocks. bookseller.

Carr, Audrey, Uppermill, teacher *r.*

Carr, Jim, Uppermill, headmaster *r.*

Carr, Stephen, Letchworth Garden City, Herts. gent.

Caunce, Dr Stephen, Arnside, Westmorland, lecturer.

Clark, Jennifer, Hill End.

Claydon, Gail, Greenfield, medical secretary.

Cline, Debra, Mechanicsburg, PA, USA.

Clough, Haydn, Grotton, laboratory technician.

Collins, Barry, Oxford, PA, USA, engineer.

Concha, Jane, Lancaster, Lancs.

Cox, Nick, Harrop Green, lecturer.

Coxon, Anthony, Grasscroft, teacher r.

Cragg, Patricia, Diggle, cook.

Crewdson, Stephen, Grasscroft, weights & measures inspector r.

Croft, Frank, Marsden, Yorks. transport manager.

Daniels, Pamela, Dale, housewife.

Delaney, Margaret, Dobcross, housewife.

Dickens, Kathryn, Portishead, Somerset, IT manager.

Douthwaite, Ian, Christchurch, New Zealand, company director.

Dyson, Dr Robert, Kenilworth, Warwicks. professor.

Entwistle, Eric, Greenfield, plumber.

Farrand, Maurice, Diggle, chartered buildings surveyor r.

Felton, Dr John, Bessacarr, Yorks. medical practicioner.

Foster, Ivan, Mossley, Lancs. joinery surveyor.

Fox, Peter, Greenfield, museum curator.

Francis, Susan, Randwick, NSW, Australia, hospital scientist.

Friedrich, Andrew, Diggle, graduate.

Friedrich, Dominic, Beswicks.

Friedrich, Julia, Beswicks, civil servant.

Friedrich, Michael F. Beswicks, joiner.

Friedrich, Michael H. Delph, farmer.

Friedrich, Nick, Diggle, graduate.

Friedrich, Richard, Beswicks, student.

Gartside, Brian, Lower Brownhill, bank manager r.

SUBSCRIBERS

Gartside, David, Fur Lane, r.

Gartside, Lorna, Hollngreave, yeoman farmer.

Gartside, Margaret, Fur Lane, r.

Glithero, Dr John, Hyde, Ches. engineer.

Grayshon, Ivy, Bucknell, Salop. civil servant r.

Griffiths, Graham, Slackcote, youth service manager.

Glynn, Michael, Oldham, Lancs. r.

Haines, David, Grasscroft, solicitor.

Halkyard, Eileen, Taunton, Somerset, typist r.

Hall, Pat, Uppermill, teacher r.

Hallowell, Michael, Ansdell, Lancs. r.

Hamilton, Ronald, Woodley, Ches. police officer r.

Hardie, Elizabeth, Delph, r.

Hawkyard, Tom, Pryors Wood, Herts. local government manager.

Higgins, Anne, Newhouses, r.

Higgins, Colin, Newhouses, r.

Hill, Amelia, Lydgate, r.

Hill, Elizabeth, Delph, community matron.

Hill, Stephen, Valenciennes, company director.

Hindes, Margaret, Uppermill, teacher r.

Hobbs, Jeffrey, Whitley Bay, Northumb. teacher.

Hodges, John, Grotton.

Holroyd, Frank, Luddington, Warwicks. r.

Houston, Linda, Golcar, Yorks.

Howarth, Anne, Aldcliffe, Lancs. r.

Howarth, Brian, Oldham, Lancs. r.

Huxley, Frank, Leiston, Suffolk, teacher r.

Isherwood, Robert, Wardle, Lancs. archaeologist.

John Rylands Library, Manchester, Lancs.

Johnson, Josephine, Greenfield, housewife.

Kenworthy, Brian, Greetham, Rutland, lecturer.

Kenworthy, Joan, Satley, Co Durham, college principal r.

Kenworthy, Robin, Staplehurst, Kent, civil servant r.

Kershaw, Donald, Southampton, Hants. chartered structural engineer r.

SUBSCRIBERS

Khadem, Victor, Ryefields, college student.

Knight, David, Grotton, building engineer.

Knight, Kathryn, Grotton, hair stylist,

Kondo, Kazuhiko, Tokyo, Japan, professor.

Knowles, Esmé, Greenfield r.

Kidd, Leonard, Greenfield, r.

Lancashire Libraries Service, Preston, Lancs.

Langton, Margaret, High Kinders.

Latimer, Sue, Kilbirnie, Ayrshire, museum curator.

Latimer, Dorothy, Lane.

Lawton, Trevor, Innaloo, WA, Australia.

McGuffie, Graham, Newhouses, school adviser.

McLintock, Susan, Burnham, Bucks.

Maloney, Terence, Dobcross, *in memoriam.*

Marcus, Chris, Shaw, Lancs. engineer.

Milnes, Peter, Scouthead, salesman.

Moseley, Janet Claire, Swansea, Glam. reseacher r.

Moore, David, Grotton, schools' bursar r.

Newby, Richard, Nicker Brow, r.

Nylan, Christine, Los Nietos, Murcia, Spain, chef.

Ogden, John, Helensburgh, Dunbs. r.

Oldham Local Studies Library, Oldham, Lancs.

Parry, Anne, Grasscroft, teacher r.

Parkin, Derek, Brownhill Naze, r.

Parkin, Nancy, Brownhill Naze, r.

Pauls, Judith, Milnrow, Lancs. r.

Petford, Alan, Hipperholme, Yorks. lecturer.

Platt, Alan, Greenfield, r.

Poole, Dr Robert, Lancaster, Lancs. lecturer.

Poole, Dr Roger, Wellington, Salop.

Poole, Yuko, Lancaster, Lancs. & Saitama, Japan.

Porisse, Marie-Thérèse, Greenfield.

Potter, Margaret, Grasscroft, headteacher r.

Price, Jean, Delph, r.

Priestley, Bert, MBE, Chadderton, Lancs. r.

SUBSCRIBERS

Quade, Anne, Woodford Green, Essex.

Robinson, Rev Jim, Ludlow, Salop. priest.

Rodgers, Mary, Delph, school clerk.

Rebneris, Vicki, Victoria, BC, Canada, secretary.

Reid, Maurice, Delph, teacher r.

Rhodes, Dr David, Wollaton, Notts. chartered engineer.

Rhodes, Jack, Delph, joiner r.

Ruddy, Charlotte, Deanhead, student.

Ruddy, Capt Chris, Deanhead, pilot.

Ruddy, Julia, Deanhead, company director.

Sakamaki, Kiyoshi, Tokyo, Japan, professor.

Sanders, Jean, Hollins, teacher r.

Scarsbook, Stephen, Denshaw, sales executive.

Schofield, Alan, Stalybridge, Ches. headteacher r.

Schofield, Dorothy, Weakey, deputy headteacher r.

Sellers, Peter, Old Tame, gent.

Shaw, Michael, Haslemere, Surrey, r.

Shaw, Melvyn, Dobcross, garage proprietor.

Shrigley, Philip, Lakewood, CO, USA, engineer.

Shrigley, Shelby, Lakewood, CO, USA, teacher.

Sigley, Karen, Diggle, tax analyst.

Smethurst, Janet, Austerlands, housewife.

Smith, W. John, Alkrington, Lancs. r.

Strange, Joyce, Birches, r.

Stott, Frances, Royton, Lancs. r.

Street, Mark, Chingford, Essex, local government officer.

Street, Robert, Holts, Lancs. r.

Sweet, Dr Rosemary, Leicester, Leics. lecturer.

Sykes, Elaine, Toronto, ON, Canada, r.

Taylor, Keith, Woolroad, lecturer r.

Tennant, Jean, Moorside, Lancs. r.

Torr, Ian, Grotton Hall, sheet metal engineer.

Toms, Geoffrey Schofield, Morley, Derbs. illustrator & teacher r.

Unsworth, Margaret, Running Hill, r.

Wareing, David, Grasscroft, r.

Wayman, Edith, Chadderton, Lancs. sheltered housing manager r.

Webster, Celia, Muswell Hill, London, child psychotherapist.

Wharton, Margaret, Delph, secretary, r.

Wheeldon, Tony, Uppermill, driver.

Wild, Alison, Mossley, Lancs.

Wild, Peter, Heyside, Lancs. tv engineer.

White, Andrew, Clapham, London, tv policy adviser.

Wilkie, Fred, Whitefield, Lancs. r.

Williams, Eileen, Eccleston, Lancs. legal personal assistant.

Wilson, Barbara, Springhead, r.

Whitehead, Alwyne, Whitecairns, Aberdeenshire, environmental advisor.

Whitehead, Clare, Linfitts, r.

Whitehead, David, Stape, Yorks. lecturer r.

Whitehead, John, Linfitts, r.

Winstanley, Dr Michael, Lancaster, Lancs. lecturer.

Wisenden, Patricia, Heights, r.

Witter, Edward, Dobcross, r.

Wood, Audrey, Delph, r.

Wood, David, Rainford, Lancs. r.

Woodhead, Geoff, Greenfield, r.

Wright, Dannie, Middleton, Lancs. Dobcross loom tuner r.

Wright, Edgar, Cricklewood, London, writer r.

Wrigley, Graham, Bexhill-on-sea, Sussex, manager r.

INTRODUCTION.

Saddleworth in the 1820s was historically almost a blank space. In these information-rich days it seems odd that a place should have no history, but (as pioneer local historians of every age know only too well) while everywhere may have a past, everywhere does not have a history until someone writes it. There was precious little to put in a history of Saddleworth except a description of a late Georgian woollen manufacturing district whose visible roots stretched no further back than the seventeenth century. What James Butterworth called "this remote part of Yorkshire" (p. 31)[1] had been the site of no great battles, movements, figures or events. It even lacked "any imposing remains of architectural grandeur". It had no obvious identity, sitting administratively in Yorkshire but topographically on the Lancashire side of the Pennines; in ecclesiastical terms it was a chapelry of Rochdale parish. It had been briefly noticed in larger histories, such as John Aikin's 1795 description of the Manchester region, but expensive works such as this were aimed at gentlemen's libraries, and unless loaned by some kind patron were virtually inaccessible to modest men such as James Butterworth, save perhaps through a visit to the ancient and ramshackle Chetham's library in Manchester. Judging by his reliance on second-hand authorities, Butterworth seems not to have made the trip. Excavations at Castleshaw had once prompted antiquarians in Manchester and Halifax to claim in respected journals that a major Roman camp had been sited in the area, but this was now a lifetime ago, and no work had been done since to support these optimistic claims.[2] Aikin had assembled a scattering of facts and figures about this "wild bleak region", including a brief mention of its Roman and "druidical" remains, while Edward Baines' 1822 *History of Yorkshire* had included a list of Saddleworth's hamlets and a few other scraps of information. But these were both contemporary descriptions rather than histories in the modern sense, and neither ran to more than four pages.[3]

The one attempt at a history of Saddleworth had been a 55-page pamphlet included with Samuel Bottomley's poem *Greenfield* in 1816. Bottomley was innkeeper at the Cross Keys in Greenfield (p.58); he died in 1795 aged 57. Aikin had seen a copy of *Greenfield*, which was first published in 1792. The poem was an attempt, as Bottomley put it, to "enrol his country in the lists of fame" by inventing a mythic past for Greenfield. It was cast in the already old-fashioned form of an epic poem laden with classical references. In 1816, after Samuel's death, one Lieutenant James Bottomley (possibly Samuel's relative) published a second edition, adding from Bottomley senior's papers a few short poems and a *History of Saddleworth*.[4] He illustrated the whole with some good quality engravings of his own. Bottomley's history was almost as overblown as the poem, starting at a vast distance in time and spending forty pages tracing Saddleworth's supposed connections with antiquity before offering a short description of the area as it stood in his own day.[5]

There was no sense of continuity between the two. Butterworth plundered Bottomley extensively, quoting sections from the poem and updating the facts and figures. He also reproduced wholesale much of the antiquarian material which Bottomley himself had simply lifted from grander works – but (as we shall see) he reworked it in interesting ways, and added his own more detailed descriptions. To the modern reader it is a curious, uneven work, and it is best understood in its whole context, starting with man who wrote it: the Oldham weaver, poet, postmaster, radical, journalist and historian James Butterworth.

JAMES BUTTERWORTH 1771-1837

James Butterworth was born in 1771 at Pitses, Alt, in the rural Medlock Vale between Oldham and Ashton-under-Lyne, within sight of Hartshead and Saddleworth itself. As one of eleven children of a weaving family, and as, himself, a weaver and the father of ten children (only three of whom survived to adulthood), Butterworth knew all about "the black and mouldy crust of poverty". He wrote feelingly of the trials of those who had to burn "the taper of diligence ... in their midnight hours, in order to procure a bare subsistence."[6] Like so many weavers, however, he found time at the loom to read and think, notwithstanding the terrible slumps that marked the French and Napoleonic wars of 1793-1815. It must have helped that he gained a regular second income as a Sunday school teacher in Mumps, Oldham, in 1799. His first publication, in 1797, was the *Draught Book*, a set of diagrams for weaving patterns, followed by an expanded edition entitled *A Guide to Universal Manufacture* (1801). He followed this with a collection of poetry, modestly titled *A Dish of Hodge Podge* (1800), an account of Masonic ideals, *The Instruments of Freemasonry Moralised* (1801), and longer poems on *Manchester* (1803) and his native *Rocher Vale* (1804). He also produced in 1798 thirteen issues of a weekly broadside miscellany, *The Manchester Political and Literary Repository*, whose main features were its clodhopping verse and its aggressive loyalism. The purpose of these early works was James' desire to show that his native people and places were fit subjects for highbrow literature and patriotic pride, and its author a worthy citizen of the powerful late-Georgian state.

In 1803 James Butterworth landed the job of postmaster for Oldham. This at last provided him with some basic security, especially once he added the roles of bookseller, fire insurance agent and tax collector. His publications, motivated by a desire for social recognition and financial solvency, promptly dried up, although the deaths of five of his children in the years 1804-10 may be sufficient explanation in itself. His duties as postmaster would have allowed him to tour the district collecting materials for his pioneering *History of Oldham*, which was published in 1817. His remarks in the preface give an idea of the difficulties of being the first historian of a district, which might equally apply to his work on Saddleworth. He complained of:

> the want of every material whereby to commence, and much more to prosecute so extensive and undertaking, which, if

managed as it ought, requires a fund if information... In every part of the work I have had to struggle with difficulties; for it seems as if the district I have here undertaken to describe, had never been much noticed by any historian.[7]

James had completed his *History of Oldham* against the background of the terrible post-war slump of 1816-17 and the rise of the radical reform movement. He seems to have been among the many supporters of the war against Napoleon who were moved by its intense privations and the disappointments of the peace to become reformers. In November 1816 Colonel Ralph Fletcher, the Bolton magistrate and spymaster, suspected that his secret correspondence with his colleague William Chippendale of Oldham was being opened at Oldham Post Office. The two men began corresponding under assumed names and the problem stopped.[8] Butterworth was suspected but no action could be taken. He was eventually dismissed in the spring of 1818 for irregularities in the accounts of the tax he collected; perhaps this radical opponent of unfair taxes was operating a Robin Hood style of assessment, leniently assessing some and over-assessing others to compensate.[9] He became a schoolteacher in Oldham, a profession he kept up until almost the end of his life, but it seems he did not give up easily on the postal service. In late 1824 the inhabitants of Lees petitioned for the Oldham-Saddleworth post to be diverted to run through Lees instead of Austerlands. The postmaster-general recommended refusal, "especially when it is considered, that the Memorial has been got up by the dismissed Receiver at Oldham, who ... has for some time past made himself busy in getting up Petitions of this sort."[10] In the 1820s, Samuel Bamford recalled, Butterworth worked as a freelance news reporter, covering Oldham and Hollinwood petty sessions.[11] Around 1829 James's youngest son Edwin, now sixteen or seventeen, began helping him with the reporting, and once he was bringing in a regular income from reporting and writing, James, now sixty, gave up writing histories. Within twelve months in 1836-7 James's wife of 44 years, his eldest son, and finally James himself, all died, leaving Edwin to struggle on to support himself and his mentally ill brother Hiram, until his own early death from overwork and ill health in 1848. The last appearance of any of the Butterworth family in the historical record was, as it happens, in Saddleworth. On 10 June 1859 Samuel Bamford was waiting to change trains at Greenfield when "I was accosted by a poor, miserable looking being who seemed suffering from hunger and other privation: he was Hiram, Edwin Butterworth's surviving brother, who had come to Saddleworth trying to sell a few clothes pegs...".[12] Edwin became a prolific chronicler and historian of Lancashire, expanding and updating many of his father's works in a more prosaic spirit. His Herculean labours and extensive manuscript collections have overshadowed those of his father, yet James was the pioneer.

James Butterworth's dismissal as postmaster gave added urgency to his writing. If the *History of Oldham* had been a labour of love for a small-town salaried official, his other histories were the work of a would-be professional writer and journalist. James had issued a revised collection of his poems, *The Rustic*

Muse, in early 1818, and followed this up in 1819 with his own version of the immensely popular comic dialect writings of Tim Bobbin, *A Sequel to the Lancashire Dialect*, written under the catchpenny pseudonym "Paul Bobbin". In 1820 he published rousing poems in the radical *Manchester Observer* in praise of the imprisoned radical Samuel Bamford and his wife Jemima, though under the pseudonym "James Ogden". Bamford only found this out later, and afterwards recalled that they were good friends for the rest of Butterworth's life.[13] It was as a chronicler of the places he knew best however that Butterworth was to make his mark.

James Butterworth's histories were of two kinds: the (mostly earlier) book-length works, and the (mostly later) pamphlets. The longer works included The *History of Oldham* (1817, expanded in 1826), *The Antiquities of Manchester* (1822-3), *A History of Ashton-Under-Lyne* (1823), expanded as *A History of Stockport, Ashton-under-Lyne, Mottram in Longdendale and Glossop* (1827) and *A History of Rochdale* (1828), to which the *History of Saddleworth* was a planned addition. Some of these works seem to have appeared in parts of about 92 pages long, issued at 3-4 month intervals with their own title pages and dedications and subsequently bound together as a book. The later pocket-sized histories by comparison were little more than a handy trade directory-cum-gazetteer with a smattering of historical background; perhaps they were intended as tasters for longer works. The pamphlets on Manchester, Salford, Bury and Stalybridge, which appeared in 1829-30, were all of 16-32 pages, but the first version of the *History of Rochdale* (36 pages, 1820) had been similar.[14] The *History of Saddleworth,* at 86 pages, came somewhere in between, and functioned both as a locally marketed booklet and as the final part of Butterworth's last book-length history. A flier and a subscription list survive among the Butterworth manuscripts. The flier announced:

> Speedily will be Published, as soon as a sufficient list of subscribers is obtained, price ten shillings and sixpence, on a superfine paper, and done up in extra boards, to contain 500 pages, octavo, embellished with an elegant view of the parish church of Rochdale, the part of Rochdale inscribed to John Entwistle, Esq. of Rochdale, and that of Saddleworth to John Radcliffe, Esq. of Stone-Breaks, Saddleworth. A complete history and description of ... Rochdale ...and Saddleworth ...

This was quite an ambitious, up-market work, and Butterworth opened a subscription list to pay for the printing.[15] Around 230 subscribers eventually paid a shilling or so deposit for their copy, but among these were only forty or so from Saddleworth and the name of the prospective dedicatee, John Radcliffe, is conspicuously absent (although his "elegant house" still got a mention in the description) (p.45). The new, young assistant curate of Saddleworth, Francis Raines, did however put down half a crown, and he and his colleague at Hey chapel duly became the dedicatees. Surviving covers indicate that the combined work was at first issued in at least thirteen smaller parts at eightpence each – not much more than the expensive newspapers of the time. Butterworth and his publisher, W. D. Varey of Manchester, seem to have struggled to raise the money for printing in small tranches, and the run of short deadlines may explain the rather rushed feel to some sections. When the full work finally appeared, the *History of Rochdale* was dated 12 September 1828, the *History of Saddleworth* 15 December. It was both sold separately and bound in with the Rochdale volume.

Why did an historian of the Lancashire cotton districts venture into Saddleworth? The prevalent opinion in Oldham, reported by Edwin a few years later, was that Saddleworth was "in another county and quite a different character from this place – the intercourse betwixt here and there is not considerable and the inhabitants of one look upon those of the other almost as foreigners". [16] It was James's only historical foray into Yorkshire, and one of the few of his father's works which Edwin did not revise. The answer lies partly in the Church. Saddleworth was technically a subordinate chapelry of Rochdale parish. As a lifelong Anglican loyalist, Butterworth naturally observed ecclesiastical boundaries – a standard format for histories in the eighteenth and nineteenth centuries. Saddleworth completed Rochdale, as well as making a useful item in its own right. There are also plenty of signs of Butterworth's own personal connections with Saddleworth. He had been born and brought up in Pitses and Alt, then (as now) in a kind of rural no-man's-land between Oldham, Ashton and Saddleworth. Hey chapel, under Ashton but serving parts of Saddleworth, would have been his local place of worship. The book, indeed, was dedicated to the Revd William Winter, who served both St Peter's, Oldham and Hey. The other dedicatee, Canon Raines, the new curate of Saddleworth, was an enthusiastic antiquarian and collector of local stories whom Butterworth must quickly have got to know – perhaps when collecting the subscriptions. Raines's access to historical sources may have been important. There is a final clue in the verse chosen by Butterworth for the title page: "O fair valley, pleasant to all my thoughts ... 'Twas here I *smarted first*, and first *knew joy!*"

WRITING THE HISTORY OF SADDLEWORTH

James Butterworth divides his *History of Saddleworth* into four parts. He opens with a general physical description of the chapelry (pp. 5-14), before entering into a long and speculative discussion of the ancient history of the area (pp. 15-31). A third part deals with the history of the Church in Saddleworth, offering some original observations (pp. 31-42). The fourth part, taking up half the book (pp. 43-83), is his detailed "topographical description" of Saddleworth as it stood in the 1820s. It is this part that is of most obvious interest to modern readers, but it is necessary to consider all four parts equally in order to appreciate how the work was put together and what it all meant.

Bottomley, as we have seen, had begun his *History of Saddleworth* with a long and fanciful account of its supposed ancient history, reaching contemporary Saddleworth only towards the end. Butterworth, by contrast, begins with the real Saddleworth – its status, situation, topography, agriculture, waterways, roads, population and general character. Most of the text of this opening section is a revised version of pages 43-53 of Bottomley – even the frontispiece engraving of Saddleworth church is a homely woodcut copy of James Bottomley's romantic copper plate. Butterworth himself adds a much fuller description of the river system and the Huddersfield canal (pp. 9-11) and a few more up-to-date facts and figures. But his rearrangement is extensive, omitting Bottomley's general history of the woollen trade to yield a much more focused account with more first-hand observation.

Butterworth's second part, his "General History of Saddleworth, from the earliest period to the present time", is also heavily indebted to Bottomley. Both men indeed are borrowers, for Bottomley in turn assembles the work of other antiquarians, but Butterworth seems to have done all his borrowing via Bottomley. The anecdote about rising land values on page 30, for example, is taken from Aikin via Bottomley (pp. 49-50), but there are no indications that Butterworth took anything from Aikin that was not used by Bottomley. The ancient history in this section is liable to strike the modern reader as an eccentric diversion. Here we are, in the middle of the industrial revolution, and instead of chronicling the immense transformation going on around them the area's first historians spend time speculating about druids and Roman roads. We need to recall, once more, where and when, Butterworth stood. Eighteenth-century history was dominated by the antiquarian search for ancient roots. The Roman remains dug up at Castleshaw and the mysteriously formed ancient stones and caverns high over Greenfield on Aldermans seemed to show deep history here in Saddleworth. It was natural for Butterworth to get excited about the opportunity to practise the most exalted historical learning using local materials.

Eighteenth-century Britain liked to see itself as a peaceful recreation of the Roman Britannia, but based more securely on peaceful trade rather than military conquest. The basic pattern of Roman roads and camps, known as the Antonine Itinerary, had been set out in William Camden's *Britannia*, a monumental Elizabethan work revised and reprinted throughout the 18th century. As Rosemary Sweet explains, "The study of Roman antiquities was something akin to a perpetual guessing game in which each antiquary attempted to join the dots of the Antonine Itinerary in such a way as would demonstrate the importance of his locality within the Roman imperium."[17] The road from Manchester, through Oldham and Saddleworth to Huddersfield, had been identified as the Roman route between Manchester and York, and Slack, near Huddersfield, as the camp of Cambodunum. Butterworth plays up Watson's and Whitaker's mid-eighteenth century case for an intermediate stop at Castleshaw in Saddleworth, and modern work has indeed confirmed Castleshaw as a fortlet established in the 70s AD and rebuilt early in the second century.[18] Butterworth pastes in quotations taken by Bottomley from two sources: John Whitaker's ponderous *History of Manchester* (1770-3) and the 1775 *History of Halifax* by the Stockport antiquarian the Revd John Watson. He is, however, careful to limit his reliance on Whitaker, whose standard work still commanded deference but which was also fanciful, error-ridden and controversial: Watson indeed had accused him of having mistranscribed a crucial inscription found at Castleshaw.[19] Whitaker had also been ridiculed in print by none other than John Collier, the Lancashire satirist "Tim Bobbin", of whom Butterworth was an admirer and who was also a friend of both Watson and Bottomley (whom he called 'cousin').[20] Butterworth's manuscripts show that he was aware that Whitaker's speculations about Roman Manchester had been criticised by none other than Samuel Johnson as "all a dream".[21]

As for the druidical material, Butterworth copies parts of an article by the Manchester antiquarian Thomas Barritt (1743-1820), again lifted via Bottomley. Barritt was a saddler of Hanging Ditch, an active member of the Manchester Literary and Philosophical Society, and another pioneer: Butterworth may have known him.[22] Barritt sought to match local details to the grandiose ideas of the well-known antiquarians William Stukeley (chronicler of Stonehenge and Avebury) and William Borlase of Cornwall. The ancient Britons and their druids were controversial. For some, they were pagan barbarians, prone to idolatry and human sacrifice, whose suppression by the civilised Romans marked the beginning of true British history and as a consequence, Christianity. But for others they were a civilised people ultimately descended from Old Testament Jewish tribes, their resistance to the Romans the foundation of British patriotism, their religion at its core simple and monotheistic, ripe for the transition to Christianity. Butterworth is in two minds about them. In his later discussion of the church, he sees the druidical period as a "dark and forbidding era" of "gloomy barbarism", dispelled by the arrival of the Christian "Light from the East" (pp. 31-2). In this second section however he favours Borlase's more benign view. The "druidical" stones at Pots and Pans are for Butterworth altars and holy water stoups, not temples of human sacrifice; the druids "acted with great justice, moderation, disinterestedness, and temperance"; and their bards were the guardians of national songs and culture. (For Butterworth the imprisoned radical and poet Samuel Bamford was a modern-day "patriot Bard").[23] At a time when Britain's governors saw themselves latter-day Roman patricians, to admire the ancient Britons who resisted them carried radical implications. In the same way, radicals admired the Saxon resistance movement to the Norman "armed banditti" (a phrase which Butterworth also uses). The romantic suggestion that the enlightened Danish King Canute might have marched through in 1017, and the theory that the language of Lancashire was essentially that of the Anglo-Saxons, fit this radical outlook nicely.[24] Butterworth is concerned at the end of this section to stress how the manor of Saddleworth existed before the Norman Conquest, and how it at had recently once more passed into the ownership of its freeholders – along with the land of Friarmere, carved out of the great abbey estates at the dissolution. Butterworth turns Bottomley's confused antiquarian jumble into a narrative of contemporary relevance, amounting to a manifesto for independence.

The independence of Saddleworth is also the theme of the third section on the Church. The importance of this section is signalled by Butterworth's dedication of the whole work to the Revd Raines of Saddleworth, and to the Revd Winter of Hey Chapel and Oldham. Francis Raines (1803-78) had just taken up his first post as assistant curate of Saddleworth, and was to spend his whole life at Rochdale and Milnrow and to become Lancashire's leading antiquarian.[25] He was well-placed to help Butterworth with sources, and probably good company for him. The dedication seems to have been well-earned, for the young George Shaw of St Chad's, Uppermill, recorded in his diary on 3 January 1829 an early reader's reaction at his grandfather's house at Stonebreaks:

> Butterworth's infamous number of Saddleworth was produced and commented upon; my Grandfather was highly indignant at the manner in which the fellow had cut up Mr Raines history, or more properly, ac[coun]t of the church of Saddleworth.[26]

It is not clear what work this would have been, for Raines has, as yet, published nothing, but his manuscripts survive in Chetham's library, Manchester, containing extensive material on the post-Restoration history of the church in Saddleworth. This part of the world nourished a vigorous popular Anglicanism, based around popular services and social activities such as Sunday schools, church music, bellringing and the annual rushbearings – rather in contrast to the received view of the Church of England in this period as decayed, worldly, remote and under-provided.[27] In Saddleworth, new chapels of ease at Friarmere (Heights Chapel, 1768), Dobcross (1787) and Lydgate (1788) were funded by local donors, which kept accommodation level with population growth.[28] In the itinerary in section 4 (pp. 64-5), Butterworth also includes Hey chapel, in Ashton parish but itself on the boundary between the two and serving a substantial part of Saddleworth. Heights (with Delph) and Lydgate even generated their own rushbearing festivals, although their flagged floors had no formal need of rushes; Dobcross fell in with Saddleworth rushbearing, and Hey with Lees. Saddleworth's old church itself had extensive free seating as well as a private west gallery, and (as Butterworth outlines) gained bells in 1781 and an organ in 1788. With regular ringings and musical recitals, with the right of marriage in the church and burial in the churchyard highly valued (not to mention the right to graze cattle there), and with the earth-floored church still the focus of annual rushbearings from all parts of the district, the established church in Saddleworth remained a popular social institution in Butterworth's day.

Part of the secret of the Church's success in Saddleworth was an easy-going clerical regime. There had been only five incumbents since the Restoration, all of them still remembered in Raines' day. The most notable of a string of eccentrics was the Revd John Heginbottom or Higinbottom (1721-71), who (Raines was told) gained the help of his parishioners to gather in his corn each year by laying on copious supplies of beer: "after the toils of harvest, 'the owd Parson' assembled his children and young neighbours who amused themselves by Dancing upon the Parsonage Green, whilst he animated their evolutions by gay and cheerful airs upon his well worn – <u>Fiddle</u>!" Heginbottom was an occasional drinking companion of the

Milnrow satirist Tim Bobbin, and once threw a chair at him across a pub. His general behaviour brought "wholesome rebukes" from the neighbouring vicar of Rochdale, the "conscientious and pious" Dr Wray.[29]

Wray's rebukes were part of a long-running dispute about Saddleworth's subjection to Rochdale parish, of which it was technically a parochial chapelry despite functioning, in effect, as a parish church. In 1714 the churchwardens of Saddleworth had asserted to the Bishop of Chester that "The Parish of Saddleworth in circumference 16 or 20 miles had within itself Parochial rights, Privileges and Liberties entire and never owed or paid to the Church of Rochdale as is common not only for Chappels of Ease but Parochial to do to their Mother Church."[30] The dispute reopened in the 1760s, and came to a head in 1771 when Richard Podmore, Wray's nominee to succeed Heginbottom, fled after being mobbed in his church when attempting to preach his first sermon, never to return. Heginbottom's popular and conscientious curate Samuel Stones took over. Podmore's successor Charles Zouch (1771-1831) was foisted on Saddleworth (perhaps in retaliation for Podmore's expulsion) despite having been removed from his previous curacy on grounds of "mental infirmity".[31] He left, after only two years, in 1794 "in consequence of his eccentricities" and was carted off to an asylum after blinding his landlady with a red-hot walking stick. (She was, incidentally, Mrs Anne Bottomley, Samuel's stepmother). Raines himself was the last and best of a series of substitutes for Zouch. His predecessor as assistant curate, John Sutcliffe (1805-28), had been "addicted to low company and drunkenness ... and never went near his school."³² The nomination issue remained live and was to be reopened in 1831.³³

Butterworth, if he knows, draws a discreet veil over all this, but his sympathies are clearly with the parishioners of Saddleworth. He modifies Bottomley's account of the various founding grants and charters of the parish, and, while conceding its historic subjection, first to Whalley and then to Rochdale, emphasises that "the patronage is unimportant" (p.36), that tithes were not paid to Whalley (p.34), that much of the eighteenth-century church building was locally funded, and that the freeholders had recently bought up the tithes (p.39). He also modifies Bottomley's date for the founding of the chapelry, based on a visit to the gatehouse of Whalley Abbey where the charters were still kept – possibly the farthest he ever ventured (p.32n). He adds his own enthusiastic description of Saddleworth church, finding virtue even in the "barbarous daub" of Daniel in the Lion's den and grandeur in the "bleak" situation and "gloomy solemnity" of the building (p.37).

Butterworth wrote towards the end of a period of change for the old church, following a visitation by Bishop Law of Chester in 1821. "It was on this visit to the old Church of Saddleworth [Raines was told] that Bishop Law observed, when turning over some Rushes which concealed the mud floor of the Nave, 'Well, Mr Church Warden, I would not lodge my Horse upon such stuff – nay, nor in your Church!'" Over the next few years, following firm orders from the Bishop, the churchyard was walled in to keep the cattle out, the burial ground extended, the floor flagged and the open benches replaced with fixed pews, followed by a virtual rebuilding in 1830-33.[34] At the time Butterworth was writing, Oldham too was in the middle of a public dispute over the renovation of its own ancient parish church, which raised similar issues of preservation, payment and authority, although the destruction of the ancient building, which Butterworth was so fond of, had not yet taken place. He seems to approve of the changes so far at Saddleworth, but his last word is for the loyal parishioners: "There are indeed few churches to be found more enthusiastically venerated by their respective attendants than Saddleworth" (p. 42). It is worth noting that this entire section of the book is about the Church of England. Butterworth postpones mention of the few dissenting chapels to the next section, looking back, perhaps, to Heginbottom's time when (Raines wrote with some exaggeration) "there was not a Dissenter in Saddleworth".

The topographical description of Saddleworth, which makes up the fourth section, is largely Butterworth's own. Even where he lifts Robinson's description of the Fairy Holes caves from Bottomley, he puts it in topographical rather than druidical context and adds his own account of a more recent exploration (pp. 53-7, cf. Bottomley pp.38-40).[35] Butterworth describes two tours: one of Lydgate, Greenfield and Dobcross (pp.44-64) and a second of Hey, Delph and Grains (pp. 64-76), and follows this with a review of other settlements outside these itineraries. The detail and richness defy easy summary; for every reader the value will be different. For Butterworth Saddleworth is a straightforwardly "romantic" landscape, with "its gently undulating valleys, its lofty and umbrageous mountains, its silvery Tame, its chrystal Diggle, and its lucid Chaw ... interesting, sublime, and magnificent", in which the smoke of Manchester and the other cotton towns is but a Turneresque detail in the distance (pp. 44-7). Repeatedly he is struck by the contrast between the "rich, varied and delightful scenery" of the valley bottoms and the "hoary grandeur" of the rocks above (pp. 50-1). Butterworth tries to assimilate Saddleworth to the kind of romantic vision that then animated travel writing about the Lake District and the Peak District. His sharply-observed description of a candle-lit exploration of the Fairy Holes and the "Devil's Cellar" near the summit of Alderman's – a "druidical retreat", he imagines – is valuable (pp. 53-7), especially when set alongside the pictorial sketches in Bottomley's *Saddleworth*.

Butterworth's account of the human settlements carefully notes the "elegant mansions", "genteel residences", "respectable shops" and accommodating public houses of his scores of subscribers, as well as the cottages, workshops, manufactories and farms where the district's wealth was generated. Here too we find useful accounts of the various dissenting chapels, respectful but significantly separated from the earlier section on the Church of England. These are first-hand descriptions. He seems to have walked virtually the whole area, just as he walked every inch of Oldham for his pioneering history of 1817. We can only regret that he did not produce a map, as he did for Oldham. (The Oldham map extends to Hey and

Austerlands). He knows even the smallest hamlets. Both Butterworth and Bottomley produced plagiarised and fanciful accounts of Saddleworth's supposed ancient past, but when it came to the present, while Bottomley's sentiments evaporated into verse, Butterworth are conveyed by close observation. To appreciate his relative thoroughness we only need to compare the formulaic list of villages in Baines' 1822 *History of Yorkshire*: Diggle "a manufacturing hamlet", Friar Mere "a large hamlet, with a chapel of ease", and so on.[36] Butterworth knew his Saddleworth, and his description is of enduring value.

The book concludes with some observations on Saddleworth's landscape and vegetation borrowed from Bottomley and an account of its people taken from Baines. This lack of originality is disappointing after what has come before. But he boldly dissents from Baines' somewhat patronising account; far from being simple and robust peasants, they are enlightened, independent and quick-witted – qualities which would stand out in any company. Butterworth's view is of a rural landscape, alternately rugged and sheltered, settled but not altered by its dozens of scattered villages and hamlets, industrious but not industrial, an "almost Elysian" region (p.51), still secluded and culturally different from the cotton towns a few miles to the west. In his own mind, this is the difference between wool and cotton, rural and urban, Pennines and plain, virtue and vice, old and new. At a time when his native Medlock Vale was becoming disfigured and polluted, it also perhaps recalled the landscape of Butterworth's own childhood in his beloved "Rocher

Vale", from where Saddleworth was (and is) a distant, enticing vision.

It has to be conceded immediately that, for all its observed detail and imaginative depth, *Saddleworth* was not one of Butterworth's major works. It was assembled with practised skill, using whatever materials came easily to hand. Crucially it was enriched by its author's personal knowledge and observation. If the emphasis on church, landscape and ancient history do not accord with our expectations of an eye-witness account of the industrial revolution, this probably says more about modern preconceptions of the period than about any inadequacies of Butterworth. Indeed, the industrial revolution, as commonly imagined, is almost absent from Butterworth's description. Even in the 1820s Saddleworth remained an overwhelmingly rural area, economically mixed, industrious rather than industrial, busy rather than business-like, dominated by natural rather than man-made landscapes, its settlements numerous, small and scattered. Outside the still-compact urban centres of Manchester and the larger cotton towns such as Oldham, much of the early industrial north-west was also like this, although cotton spinning was more mechanised than Saddleworth's woollens. Visitors go to Manchester to see the remains of the industrial revolution, but Manchester has changed out of all recognition while Saddleworth remains a much better example of an early industrial landscape. Butterworth is a witness to that.

Butterworth's book reflects its period in another way, albeit a less expected one. His interest in myth, ancient history, archaeology, landscape, custom, and popular Anglicanism were part of the romantic antiquarian revival of the 1820s. In this decade the medieval walls of York were restored, the historical novels of Walter Scott were the publishing sensation of the day, Scottish highland traditions were manufactured to welcome George IV to Edinburgh, folklore began to be collected and published both by Tories such as John Roby (in his 1829 *Traditions of Lancashire*) and radicals such as William Hone (in several editions of his *Yearbook*). The 1820s also brought a new wave of local histories which sought to record the rapid progress of their districts at the same time as connecting them with the deeper past. A digital age, which is also enjoying a boom in television history, needs no reminding that an interest in the past is just as valid a response to rapid change as the worship of progress. James Butterworth wrote pioneering histories of the manufacturing districts, Saddleworth included, which sought to embrace both progress and the past. In this, too, he was very much the product of his age.

Robert Poole
St Martin's College, Lancaster

FOOTNOTES TO THE INTRODUCTION

[1] Numbers in brackets refer to the original page numbers of Butterworth's *History of Saddleworth*.

[2] Thomas Percival, "Observations on the Roman stations in Lancashire", *Philosophical Transactions of the Royal Society of London* xlvii (1751); J. Watson, "Some account of a Roman station lately discovered on the borders of Yorkshire", *Archaeologia* i (1766). Here and at other places I am indebted to Neil Barrow for references and local information.

[3] John Aikin, *A Description of the Country from Thirty to Forty Miles Around Manchester* (London, 1795), pp. 556-9; Edward Baines, *History, Directory and Gazetteer of the County of York I: West Riding* (Leeds, 1822), pp. 262-5.

[4] Samuel Bottomley had been born in 1738, and James c.1767. James' obituary notice read: "Died at Cheetwood near Manchester Mar 15th 1840 aged 73 James Bottomley, late of the 15th Foot well known for the many engraved views of various localities engraved by him." WEA Axon, *The Annals of Manchester: A Chronological record from the earliest times to the end of 1885* (Manchester, 1885) and "Lydgate: an Interesting Sketch", *Oldham Standard* 30 Aug. 1924.

[5] Samuel Bottomley, *Greenfield: a Poem* 2nd edn, (Manchester, 1816) Manchester Central Library 942.74 S16. Manchester Central Library's card catalogue attributes the *History* to James Bottomley, while another card misattributes a first (undated) edition of the poem to him. The history does contain post-1795 information, which at least must have been added by James. But he wrote in the preface to the 1816 edition, 'I am sufficiently convinced of the truth of the following Description', suggesting that he himself had not written it. Samuel

Bottomley's historical interests emerge in his correspondence with 'Tim Bobbin' (see below n.20).

[6] James Butterworth, An *Historical and Descriptive Account of the Town and Parochial Chapelry of Oldham in the County of Lancaster* (Oldham, 1817), Preface. For a full account of James Butterworth's life, see R. Poole and M. Winstanley, *The Butterworths of Oldham* (Carnegie Press/Manchester Centre for Regional History, forthcoming 2006). For an earlier account, see Giles Shaw, "James Butterworth of Oldham", *Transactions of the Lancashire and Cheshire Antiquarian Society* xxvi (1908).

[7] James Butterworth, *An Historical Account...of Oldham*, (Oldham, 1817) Preface.

[8] National Archives, Public Record Office (PRO) HO40/3 (Part 5) fols. 935-40; HO41/1 fol. 489.

[9] Post Office archives, Mount Pleasant, POST 42/105 [vol. 33], pp. 367, 408, 461 (reports nos. 256, 293, 346); POST 42/106 p. 44 (report no. 157).

[10] POST 24/111 p. 540 (report no. 673).

[11] *Oldham Chronicle* supplement, 9 April 1859.

[12] *The Diaries of Samuel Bamford*, ed. M. Hewitt and R. Poole (Stroud, 2000), 10 June 1859.

[13] *Manchester Observer* 10 June 1820, 8 July 1820.

[14] *A Chronological Table of the History of Manchester* (Manchester, 1829), *A Gazetteer of the Hundred of Salford* (Manchester, 1830), *History of Bury* (Manchester, 1829) and *History of Stalybridge* (1831, unpublished in his lifetime).

[15] Butterworth mss, Oldham Local Studies and Archives (OLS), D-BUT/K/B3.

[16] Edwin Butterworth Newsbooks, OLS, 10 January 1837.

[17] Rosemary Sweet, *Antiquaries* (London, 2004), p. 171 and ch. 5 generally.

[18] J. Walker (ed.), *Castleshaw: The Archaeology of a Roman Fortlet*, Manchester 1989; Ken Booth, *Roman Saddleworth*, Saddleworth Archaeological Trust 2001, and see note 2. The "wall of Severus" (p. 25) was the then name for Hadrian's Wall. My thanks to David Shotter of Lancaster University for assistance on these points: see D. Shotter, *The Romans in North West Britain*, 4th edn (Centre for North-West Regional Studies, Lancaster University, 2004).

[19] John Watson, *History of Halifax* (1775), pp. 40-42.

[20] "Muscipula" (John Collier), *Curious Remarks on the History of Manchester* (1771) and *More Fruit from the Same Pannier* (1773), both in H. Fishwick (ed.), *Works of Tim Bobbin* (Rochdale, 1890); John Collier to [Samuel] Bottomley, 14 Dec. 1780, in Henry Fishwick (ed.), *The Works of John Collier* (Rochdale, 1894), pp. 297-8; R. Poole, "John Collier (Tim Bobbin)", *Oxford Dictionary of National Biography* (2004). For a broader and more positive assessment of Whitaker, see Sweet, *Antiquaries*, pp. 20-1, 173, 177-9, 412n.

[21] Butterworth papers, OLS, D-BUT/H/2/4.

[22] Alan G. Crosby, "Thomas Barritt", *Oxford Dictionary of National Biography* (Oxford, 2004).

[23] *Manchester Observer* 10 June 1820, 8 July 1820, writing as "John Ogden".

[24] All this is taken from Bottomley, and the Canute theory is in turn borrowed from Robert Plot's seventeenth-century *The Natural History of Staffordshire (London, 1686)*.

[25] C. W. Sutton (revised Alan G. Crosby), "Francis Raines", *Oxford Dictionary of National Biography* (Oxford, 2004).

[26] Diary of George Shaw, Manchester Central Library archives MS 927.2 S15 (now in Oldham Local Studies and Archives, acc 2005-294).

[27] Mark Smith, *Religion in Industrial Society: Oldham and Saddleworth 1740-1865* (Oxford, 1994), especially ch. 2, and his

"The Reception of Richard Podmore", in J. D. Walsh, C. Haydon and S. Taylor (eds), *The Church of England 1689-1833* (Cambridge, 1993). The debate over the health or otherwise of the state of the church in this part of the world is explored in a lively exchange between Smith and Michael Snape over Snape's book *The Church of England in Industrialising Society: The Lancashire Parish of Whalley in the Eighteenth Century* (Woodbridge, 2003) on the *Reviews in History* website at www.history.ac.uk. The debate is not easily resolved, for the popularity of the Church in Saddleworth appears to have owed much to local resistance to ecclesiastical authority in Rochdale and beyond.

[28] Raines mss ii.97-8, Chetham's Library, Manchester; Smith, *Religion in Industrial Society*, pp. 34-40.

[29] Raines mss i.273-8; Fishwick, *Works of Tim Bobbin*, pp. 297-8; Giles Shaw mss i.67-8 OLS.

[30] Raines mss xv. 30-1.

[31] John Radcliffe (ed.), *The Parish Registers of St Chad, Saddleworth vol. 2: (Uppermill,* 1887), p.540.

[32] Giles Shaw mss i.116.

[33] Raines mss i.277-8; Smith, "Reception of Richard Podmore".

[34] Raines mss i.165 ; ii.99-100, 187 ; xv.212. For a sketch of the churchyard in 1828 see Raines mss xiii.260. This can be compared with the slightly earlier rushbearing scene in Alfred Burton, *Rushbearing* (Manchester, 1890), reproduced in A. J. Howcroft, *The Chapelry and Church of Saddleworth* (Oldham, 1915), p. 57.

[35] For engraving and plan of the caverns, see Bottomley, *Greenfield,* facing pp. 9 and 31.

[36] Edward Baines, *History, Directory and Gazetteer of the County of York I: West Riding*, pp. 262-5.

A LIST

OF THE SUBSCRIBERS TO THIS WORK.

JOHN ENTWISLE, Esq.
JOHN CROSSLEY, Esq. } PATRONS.
JOHN ELLIOTT, Esq.

JAMES BUCKLEY, Esq. Holly Ville, Saddleworth,
Rev. F. R. RAINES, Curate of Saddleworth,
JOHN LEE, Esq. Rochdale,
Rev. WILLIAM WINTER, Oldham,
JAMES GEE, Esq. Hollinwood House,
Rev. J. SELKIRK, A. M. Ashworth Hall,
Rev. R. SINGLETON, Blackley,
Rev. JOSEPH COWELL, Todmorden,
Rev. HERBERT ALLKIN, Lydgate, Saddleworth,
JOHN HARROP, Esq, Dobcross,
WM. NEWALL, Esq. Wellington Lodge,
JOHN FIELDEN, Esq. Dawson Hall, near Todmorden,
ISAAC BALL, Esq. Rochdale,
WM. MIDGLEY, Esq. near Rochdale,
WILLIAM HASSAL, Esq. Bolderstone,
WILLIAM MANN, Esq. Larkfield,
JOHN MIDGLEY, Esq. Deeplish hill,
Rev. WM. HODGSON, Church Cottage,
Rev. GEORGE DODDS, Drake Street,
T. S. RAWSON, Esq. Rochdale,
JOHN RADCLIFFE, Esq. Stonebreaks, Saddleworth,
JOHN ROBERTS, Esq. Delph,

SUBSCRIBERS' NAMES.

Mr. Joseph Taylor, Yeoman, Shelderslow.
Rev. Bowness Cleasby, near Appleby.
Mr. Joseph Battye, Solicitor, Rochdale.
Mr. Adam Fletcher, Greenacres Moor.
Mr. James Scholfield, Surgeon, Middleton.
Mr. Charles Harrop, Manufacturer, Dobcross.
Mr. Booth Harrop, Ditto.
Mr. J. Radley, Solicitor, Oldham.
Mr. Edwd. Baines, Printer, Leeds.
Mr. Edmund Buckley, Canal Warehouse, Manchester.
Mr. James Taylor, Walkers, Saddleworth.
Mr. James Dixon, Hathershaw.
Mr. John Nuttall, Yorkshire Street.
Mr. Thos. Bailey, Rochdale.
Mr. Thos. Shaw, New Delph.
Mr. R. J. Halsall, Solicitor, Middleton.
Mr. Wm. Taylor, Surgeon, Royton.
Mr. H. Whitehead, Solicitor, Rochdale.
Mr. Richd. Hunt, Ditto Ditto.
Mr. J. Buckley, Surgeon, Rochdale.
Mr. A. Scholfield, Manufacturer Milnrow.
Mr. John Butterworth, near Milnrow.
Mr. John Clough, Painter, Rochdale.
Mr. Abrm. Milne, New Hey.
Mr. Edmund Lord, Lower Mill.
Mr. John Stott, Bent House.
Mr. H. Race, Town House.
Mr. John Stott, near Littlebro'.
Messrs. John Haworth & Son, Rochdale.
Betty Cure, Ditto.
Messrs. Jas. and Jno. Milne, Burnage.
Mr. Joseph Radcliffe, Drake Street.
Mr. Samuel Holland, Packer Street.
Mr. Charles Slade, Rochdale.
Mr. Wm. Kite, South Parade, Rochdale.
Mr. Aaron Collier, Dukinfield.
Mr. Richd. Redfern, Dobcross.
Mr. Wm. Beaumont, Austerlands.
Mr. John Buckley, Manufacturer, Todmorden.
Rev. James Ousey, do.
Mr. Thomas Thomas, do.
Mr. James Holt, do.
Mr. George Eccles, do.
Mr. Heyworth Heyworth, do.
Mr. Edmund Wrigley, do.

SUBSCRIBERS' NAMES.

Mr. Abraham Barker, Todmorden.
Mr. Abraham Horsfall, do.
Mr. Thos. Edwd. Hammerton, Solicitor, do.
Mr. Henry Taylor, Rochdale.
Mr. Hugh Oldham, Schoolmaster, do.
Mr. Edward Lees, Saddleworth.
Mr. James Taylor, Great Yates.
Mr. John Kershaw, Schoolmaster, Lower Place.
Mr. Robt. Scholfield, Shopkeeper, do.
Mr. Henry Stealey, Rochdale.
Mr. David Newland, do.
Rev. John Ely, Providence Chapel.
Mr. Samuel Stott, Rochdale.
Mr. Wm. Petre, do.
Mr. James Midgley, Springhill.
Mr. Jas. Greenwood, Academy, Drake Street.
Mr. Jeffery Baron, Drake street
Mr. J. Redfern, Yorkshire Street.
Mrs. Cooke, Ladies' School, Summer Castle.
Mr. Jesse Rothwell, Druggist, Rochdale.
Mr. Walter Dunlop, Surgeon, Rochdale.
Mr. Edmund Ogden, Blue Ball, Rochdale.
Mr. Richd. Sellers, Rochdale.
The Book Society, Dog, Milnrow.
Mr. Henry Kelsall, Rochdale.
Mr. W. Dunlop, Jun. Rochdale
Mr. Chas. Milne, Drake Street, Rochdale.
Mr. Jno. Lamb, Moor Street, do.
Mr. John Erving, George Street, Rochdale.
Mr. James Hopwood, Yorkshire Street, do.
Mr. Wm. Shepherd, Citizen, Drake Street, do.
Mr. Octavius Augustus Lee, do.
Mr. John Cropper, Hope Street Rochdale.
Mr. Benjamin Shaw, Packer, Meadow, do.
Mr. James Taylor, do. do.
Mr. Thomas Chadwick, Drake Street, do.
Mr. James Gibson, do. do.
Mr. Samuel Taylor Holt, Packer Street, do.
Mr. Edmund Percival, Butts, Ditto.
Mr. Joshua Radcliffe, Drake Street, do.
Mr. Robert Crossley, Drake Street, do.
Mr. John Athinson, Yorkshire Street, do.
Mr. James Tweedall, Corn Merchant, Cheetham Street, do.

SUBSCRIBERS' NAMES.

Messrs. Joseph Heap & Sons, Yorkshire Street, Rochdale
Mr. Henry Cartwright, do. do.
Mr. Thos. Howden, 50 copies, ditto.
Mr. James Shepherd, Yorkshire Street, do.
Mr. Benjn. Butterworth, do.
Mr. Wm. Littlewood, Academy ditto.
Mr. James Butterworth, Manufacturer, Yorkshire Street ditto.
Mr. Edmund Butterworth, Parade Street, do.
Mr. Benjamin Butterworth, Black Water Street, do.
Mr. William Heaton, Solicitor, ditto.
Mr. James Holloday, do.
Mr. George Ashworth, Holland Street, do.
Mr. J. Ogden, Surgeon, Yorkshire Street, do.
Mr. W. Law, Schoolmaster, Drake Street, do.
Mr. James Shaw, Yorkshire Street, do.
Mr. Sutcliffe, Surgeon, do.
Mr. John Mason, Machine Maker, Bell Street, do.
Mr. Jas. Woods, Solicitor, Yorkshire Street, do.
Mr. Thomas Fisher, Cheetham Street, do.
Mr. William North, Yorkshire Street, Rochdale.
Mr. James Atkinson, Schoolmaster, do.
Mr. William Marsden, Cheetham Street, do.
Mr. G. Alexander, MD. do.
Mr. John Webster, Commercial Inn, do.
Miss Jane Buckley, Gorton.
Mr. John Shaw, Hosier, Stayley Bridge.
Mr. Cornelius Goddard, Stayley Wood.
Mrs. Mills, Park House, Crompton.
Mr. Jas. Holt, George Street, Oldham.
Mr. John Thorp, Glossop.
Mr. Samuel Wrigley, Scout Head, Saddleworth.
Mr. John Shaw, Grocer, Dobcross.
Mr. Benjamin Buckley Fox, Painter, Gilder, &c. Upper Mill.
Mr. William Haigh, Innkeeper, Shaw Hall.
Mr. Thos. Shaw, Grottenhead.
Mr. Jas. Kenworthy, Quick.
Mr. John Hilton, Quick.
Mr. Thos. Wrigley, Lydgate.
Mr. Wm. Whitehead, Grass Croft.
Mr. C. R. Stephens, do.

SUBSCRIBERS' NAMES.

Mr. Thos. Bebbington, Grass Croft.
Mr. George Adshead, Upper Mill.
Mr. Giles Shaw, do.
Mr. Joseph Lawton, Attorney, Delph.
Mr. James Kenworthy, Grass Croft.
Mr. James Wright, do.
Mr. Jno. Buckley, High Grove
Mr. William Broadbent, Saddleworth Fold.
Mr. John Platt, near do.
Mr. Chas. Harrop, Dobcross.
Mr. James Platt, Schoolmaster, Boarshurst.
Mr. Robt. Shaw, near do.
Mr. Samuel Heginbottom, Surgeon, Upper Mill.
Mr. Francis Platt, do.
Mr. Ammon Platt, do.
Mr. Richard Brockbank, Wool Road.
Mr. Robt. Winterbottom, do.
Mr. Benjamin Wrigley, New Houses.
Mr. John Haigh, Spring Hill.
Mr. Wm. Lawton, Shelderslow
Mr. John Buckley, do.
Mr. John Robinson, Wood Brook.
Rev. John Holroyd, Delph.
Mr. Alexander Thoms, Surgeon Delph.
Mr. John Gartside, Grocer, Junction.
Mr. James Whitehead, Jun. do.
Mr. William Waring, Street Cut, near Grains.
Mr. James Wrigley, Lydgate.
Mr. John Bradbury, Kinders.
Mr. Joseph Harrop, Grass Croft
Mr. James Scholfield, do.
Mr. Jas. Bottomley, Greenfield.
Mr. Wm. Harrison, Thornley.
Mary Bottomley, Cross Keys, Saddleworth Church.
Mr. Hugh Brierley, Dobcross.
Mr. Josiah Lawton, Innkeeper, ditto.
Mr. John Kenworthy, Surgeon, ditto.
Mr. Wm. Warhurst, Nudger Inn, Dobcross.
Miss Hannah Booth, Coach and Horses, Waterhead Mill.
Mr. Edward Smith, Packer, Rochdale.

N. B. *An additional List of Subscribers will be given in the Appendix.*

A

LIST OF THE SUBSCRIBERS

Obtained since the commencement of this Work.

The Rev. J. GAITSKELL, Curate of Whitworth.
The Rev. JOHN BUCKLEY, Curate of Friar Mere.
R. & R. SHUTTLEWORTH, Esqrs. Rochdale.
Mr. Wm. Harrison, Coverhill, near Lydgate.
,, Joseph Broadbent, Marslands, Saddleworth.
,, John Broadbent, Carr, do.
Mrs. Alice Broadbent, Marslands, do.
Mr. Benjamin Broadbent, Dobcross.
,, Wm. Eastwood, Walk Mill, do.
,, Johu Buckley, Carr Hill, near Mossley.
,, Samuel Stott, Canal Wharf, Rochdale.
,, Charles Francis Rhodes, Bell Street, do.
,, John Radcliffe, Boars Hurst, Saddleworth.
,, John Bebbington, Upper Mill, do.
,, John Wrigley, Banker, Dobcross, do.
,, Thos. Garratt, Wool Road, do.
,, Robt. Chadwick, Shaw Clough, near Rochdale.
,, James Butterworth, Wool Merchant, do.

SUBSCRIBERS.

Mr. James Milne, Primrose Hill, near Shaw.
,, Robert Wrigley, Hamer Cottage, near Rochdale.
,, James Newton, Coach Maker, Rochdale.
,, John Winterbottom, Agent to the Colliery, Oldham.
,, James Clegg, Loeside, near Oldham.
Mrs. Hannah Whitehead, Heights Lane, near Rochdale.
Mr. Charles Harwar, Oldham.
,, Thomas Becket, Glodwick, near Oldham.
,, Thomas Wrigley, Shelderslow, Saddleworth.
,, John Reistrick, Wool Road, do.
,, Robt. H. Williamson, Druggist, Delph, do.
,, Robt. Platt, Shopkeeper, Hey Chapel.
,, John Whitworth, Church Style, Rochdale.
,, T. Sladin, Free School, Littleborough.
,, J. Booth, Druggist, Rochdale.
,, Wm. Kenworthy, Dyer, Thornley, near Lees.

SADDLEWORTH CHURCH.

A HISTORY AND DESCRIPTION

OF THE

𝔓𝔞𝔯𝔬𝔠𝔥𝔦𝔞𝔩 𝔈𝔥𝔞𝔭𝔢𝔩𝔯𝔶

OF

SADDLEWORTH,

IN THE COUNTY OF

YORK.

O fair valley, pleasant to all my thoughts,
Pleasant as drink to parched thirsty souls,
Pleasant as shade in burning Torrid Clime,
Or downy pillow, to the weary limb
Of worn out traveller, or toilsome serf,
'Twas here I *smarted first*, and first *knew joy!*

BY JAMES BUTTERWORTH.

MANCHESTER:
Printed by W. D. VAREY, 3, Red Lion Street, St. Ann's Square.
1828.

Dedication.

To the REV. F. R. RAINES, Assistant Curate of Saddleworth,

AND TO

The REV. WM. WINTER,

Incumbent of Hey Chapel, and of St. Peter's, Oldham,

This attempt, at a History and Description,

OF

THE PAROCHIAL CHAPELRY

OF

SADDLEWORTH,

Is with all due submission, humbly inscribed, by

Rev. Gentlemen,

Your obedient, humble, and devoted Servant,

JAMES BUTTERWORTH.

BUSK, near Oldham,
December 15th, 1828.

Parochial Chapelry of Saddleworth.

This district comprises a mountainous though in some parts pleasant and romantic country, situate at the south west angle of the extensive county of York, and in the Wapentake of Agbrigg, though it is included in the parish of Rochdale, in the county of Lancaster. Saddleworth is bounded by the rest of the parish of Rochdale on the north, the Parochial Chapelry of Oldham on the west and north west, the parish of Ashton-under-Line on the south west, all of which districts are in Lancashire; the parish of Mottram-in-long-den-dale, in Cheshire, on the south and south east, and by the parish of Huddersfield on the east. The village of Saddleworth, (commonly called Saddleworth Fold,) nearly in the centre of the district, is distant from Oldham, in Lancashire, six miles, east south east, twelve miles from Huddersfield, west south west, thirteen miles from Manchester, east north east, twelve miles from Rochdale, south south east, seven miles from Ashton-under-Line, north east, and two hundred miles, north north west, from London. These hills, (of which the range of Saddleworeh are a part,) extend in a line upwards of two hundred miles, those of Blackstone-Edge being part of this said mountainous ridge. Saddleworth is placed in an angle of Yorkshire, betwixt Lancashire and the north eastern projection of Cheshire.

This Chapelry is large and extensive, being upwards of eight and a half miles in length, from north to south, and about five and a half in breadth, from west to east. It is of a long irregular shape. Upon the whole, Saddleworth is an interesting though uninviting part of the country, presenting to the eye of the observer, a district interspersed with high and barren hills and fertile vallies ; the most rich and luxuriant part is the vale stretching up towards Greenfield. The soil of this part of the parish (Rochdale,) is rich and loamy in some places, in others it partakes more of the clay. The land lets chiefly in small farms, principally keeping from one to three head of cattle thereon, the rental generally between two and three pounds per acre. The sheep are of the middle size. Gardening is not so much attended to, though there are many of the inhabitants who have a taste for Horticulture. Here is plenty of good stone, both for building and making of fences. The most ancient way of erecting buildings in these parts was of wood and clay, as appears from several instances, but the timber trees which composed the *general forest*, in which this gloomy district was wholly comprehended and inclosed, being now nearly all cut down, and little or no care taken to plant afresh, recourse has been had to stone, which is very durable, and when properly worked has a very good appearance, but when polished and every external beauty exhibited, it is attended with very considerable expence. Coal is a scarce article, and what is obtained is very trifling, it is therefore chiefly brought by the canal from the neighbouring townships of Oldham, Dukinfield, Crompton, &c. Lime is obtained from the Peak of

Derbyshire. Turf is very plentiful here, among the hills, and when cut and dried in summer forms a good substitute for coal.

Amongst the barren moorlands of Saddleworth grow abundance of whinberries, cranberries, bilberries, cloudsberries, and crowberries, the getting of which employs many of the juvenile part of the population of this district in the summer months. In the mosses are frequently found parts of trees of different dimensions, which evidently prove (were there no historical data,) that this region was, not very many centuries ago, one unreclaimed forest. On the hills are grouse and moor game, for the amusement of the sportsman. Oats are the general bread of this district and the vicinity, as they were of the whole kingdom in the time of the conquest, and the cakes made here are excellent in their kind, but wheaten bread is getting much into use, particularly in the villages and more populous parts of this place.

"The way of preparing the ground (in Saddleworth,) for the reception of the seed," which produces the staff of life, "is not always by ploughing, but very frequently by what is called *graving*, which is performed by one man cutting the ground in a right line to a certain depth with a spade contrived for the purpose, and another pulling the earth over with an instrument called a *Hack*, and so making a furrow. This is the only method which can be used on the very steep sides of some hills. There is nothing remarkable in the reaping of corn here, but a good part of it as well as the hay, is carried in on the shoulders of men, on account of the difficulties of carriages moving up and down the steep declivities of the mountains, and the inhabitants of these hilly parts are so very dexterous at this work, that it appears to be the most expeditious method, either when the ground is very uneven or the distance but small. One substantial reason however why this practice, as well as graving, are so general, is the scarcity of draught horses, those which are kept being so employed about trade, that they can seldom be spared for hssbandry."

Bottomley.

The air of Saddleworth is excellent and healthy, as well as the rest of this large parish, as will be seen in the judicious observations of Mr. Watson. The following is a singular proof of the healthiness of the district; a benefit society was established in this tract we are describing, in 1772, consisting of 300 members, some of whom at their entrance were more than fifty years of age, and only twelve members had been buried out of it, to the beginning of 1794.

Saddleworth, as before observed, is one continued range of hills and vallies, some of which are very high and steep, particularly those of Harrop Edge, Stand Edge, Pule, Alderman, Alphin, Brunn, and Warmton. To enumerate however every hill and eminence, would extend beyond our limits. Level ground is scarcely any where found in this tract, except on the tops of the hills, or in the very depths of the vallies. Snow is seen on these mountains sometimes in May, and it is even cold on the summit of some of these hills, when it is quite warm and pleasant at the bottom. Saddleworth may be considered as one large valley, commenciug at Brook-Bottom, near Mossley, and extending all along, (though with various lesser and collateral branches stretching therefrom in different directions,) to above the Junction Inn. Saddleworth is divided into four townships, here named meres, (the ancient term for boundary,) namely *Quick Mere*, this includes the south west part thereof; *Friar's Mere*, the north east part of the district; *Shaw Mere*, the south east; and *Lord's Mere* the west. Friar's Mere was anciently an estate belonging to the Black Friars, who had, (it is said) a house or grange therein, near Delph. Streams, and springs of the purest water, are numberless in this district, as almost every field, every hamlet, and every little valley has its beck or brook, so that the united waters of these numberless rills, swell the Tame to a very considerable stream before it disembouges from the valley. The rivers Tame, Chaw, Diggle, and Hull Brook owe their formation to these rills and rivulets, and the abundance of water has caused the erection of manufactories, and various mills, throughout the whole extent of this district; the river Tame rises at the foot of some hills, near Blackstone Edge, and passes Denshaw, Tame, Linfits, and Delph, where it is joined by Hull Brook; it then pours its waters by New Delph, and sweeping along by the place named Tame Water, and Brown Hill, where the Diggle empties itself into it, and then passing Upper Mill; below French Mill the Chaw disembouges its slender stream thereinto; it then winds along by Stayley, separating Cheshire from Lancashire, Stayley Bridge, Dukinfield, Ashton-under-Lyne, Audenshaw, Denton, Hyde, Wernith, Houghton, Bredbury, Brinnington, and at Portwood Bridge, in Stockport, it discharges itself into the Mersey, forming from Stayley the division or boundary line of the counties of Cheshire and Lancashire, all along to Stockport. The Chaw rises in the hills above Greenfield, and falls into the Tame near French's mill, as before stated. The Diggle rises above Dig Lee, and pouring its stream through Harrop Dale, falls into the more majestic Tame at Brownhill. Hull Brook has its source amongst the arid hills and gullies, in and about Friar's Mere, joining the winding Tame at Delph; three of the first Dr. Whitaker says are pure British names, but of this we shall speak more fully in the historical records of this district. A considerable branch of the *Medlock* rises near High Moor, in Saddleworth, and flowing in a south easterly direction is joined by a smaller branch of the same, descending from near Quick Edge, these unite their waters near Spring Head, and fall into a larger branch of the Medlock, at Holts, in Knott Lane, in the parish of Ashton-under-Lyne.

The Huddersfield Canal. The Act for executing this line of canal navigation, passed in April, 1794. Its two extremities are the Ashton-under-Lyne canal, on the western side, and Sir John Ramsden's canal, to the river Calder, at the town of Huddersfield, in the county of York, on the eastern. Its general direction is north east. From Ashton-under-Lyne it takes its course parallel to the river Tame, often crossing the mazy windings thereof; above Stayley Bridge, and at Carr Hill it enters Yorkshire, in the mountainous though manufacturing district of Saddleworth, which by the greater facility of conveyance, it has very considerably enriched. From Carr Hill it pursues its course over the Tame, by an acqueduct of two arches, which is situate below Grove, from hence it reaches the improving and populous village of Upper Mill, to the north of which it passes Wool Road, where a large warehouse has been erected for the reception of goods, to the east of Wool Road, it arrives at its head level and penetrates the high grounds, by a tunnel 5477 yards, or three miles and 197 yards in length, passing beneath Pule Moss, and emerging from its subterranean passage under these lofty mountains near Marsden; from whence it proceeds by Slaithwaite to Huddersfield, closely accompanying and often crossing the river Colne. Its extreme length is 19 miles and three quarters; it passes through Saddleworth about three miles, exclusive of the tunnel; its fall from the head level is 436 feet, on the Huddersfield side, and 334 feet 8 inches on the Ashton-under-Lyne side. Several of the little rills and mountain streams are expanded into small reservoirs, for the supply of its water. The tunnel of this canal is the most stupendous work of the kind in England, and is said by some to be nearly four miles long. This navigation which penetrates through the centre of Saddleworth, has conferred a lasting benefit on this district, and greatly facilitated the transition from place to place, of coal, lime, wool, slate, manures, &c. It connects the populous towns of Huddersfield, Ashton-under-Lyne, and Manchester with each other, and indeed every town on the line of the same from Liverpool to Hull.

There are many excellent *Turnpike Roads* through Saddleworth, leading to and from the principal towns of the surrounding country, the chief of which are the

Wakefield and Oldham road, which traverses through the whole breadth of Saddleworth. The Stockport and Doctor Lane road runs about three miles through, and the Oldham and Stanedge road, passing through Upper Mill, (with two branches one from Shaw Hall to Hollins, end another from Wallhill to Woolroad,) extends about six miles, and the two branches about two miles each. The Oldham and Ripponden road, (with two branches, one from Junction to Delph, and another from Grains to Delph,) runs through this district about three miles, the two branches about two miles each. The Stayley Wood and Brookhouses road, with a branch from Stayley Bridge to Shaw Hall passes about one mile through the district. The Huddersfield and New Hey road extends about three miles through. Before these turnpike roads existed the roads were very bad, and some of them were scarcely passible for carriages or carts. The principal one was from Stanedge to a place called Lee-Cross, passing Saddleworth Parochial Chapel, Knowltop to Lanehead Cross, and then forward by the side of the hills below Bucton Castle, to a place Roe Cross, near Mottram-long-den-dale, thence forward into Derbyshire. This is one of the ancient roads called the Old Romam Road. Another old road from Stanedge through Saddleworth, was by Delph, Knotthill Lane, Hill Top, Thurston Clough, High Moor, and Waterhead Mill, to Oldham. Another road extending from Stanedge over Harrop Edge, to Dobcross, Lydgate, and Quick Edge, Brookbottom and Mossley, to Ashton-under-Lyne. These ancient roads were regularly travelled by pack-horses, to and from the neighbouring towns.

Villages. Saddleworth is said to contain no less than seventy-two distinct villages and hamlets; the principal villages are Upper Mill, Dobcross, Delph, Blakehey Nook, Wool Road, and Brookbottom. And Diggle Bridge, Boarshurst, Grass Croft, Lydiate and Springhead may be considered as the principal hamlets, of this flourishing district.

The *Population* of Saddleworth has been amazingly on the increase since the introduction of manufactures and trade, these being a stimulus to population and improvements; the population of the chapelry in 1801, was 1065; in 1811 it had increased to 12579, and in 1321 it had further swelled to the number of 13902. According to Bottomly, at the time he wrote in 1816, there were then 400 freeholders in Saddleworth, and (he adds,) it is stated to contain 1822 families.

Employment. The woollen manufactures of this district gives employment to a majority of the inhabitants; the spinning of cotton also of late years employs a considerable number of those who formerly were only acquainted with the woollen branch. Agriculture also employs a few, but comparatively speaking, but a small number of its present population.

The *Manufactures* of Saddleworth are principally woollen cloths, and there are numerous mills erected throughout the district, where all the operations necessary for preparing and manufacturing the goods are performed, which now for excellence vie with those of the west of England. Woollens were formerly the produce of Flanders, and other foreign countries, till our wise Edward the Third issued an edict, inviting cloth workers over here. Aikin in his history of from twenty to forty miles round Manchester, states, "In 1740, there were not more than 8640 cloths manufactured in Saddleworth, and those of a very course kind; in 1791 the number was 35,639; and in 1792, (when he published his work,) there were 36,637, which at an average were worth £7 each, in an unfinished state, and sold at Huddersfield market. For the manufacturing of these cloths, (saith he,) are used 1,480,000 lbs of wool; the number of looms are about 2000, and there are seventy six mills turned by the Tame, and the smaller streams falling thereinto. These manufactures extend throughout the whole of the district, and probably originally spread here from Rochdale. In 1820 the number of pieces milled, according to the supervisors accounts or returns, amounted to 7,026 narrows, and 12,458 broads, exclusive of kerseymeres and shawls, which have been the principal goods manufactured here of late years, and of which there were produced in this chapelry during the year 1824, 40,000 pieces. The cotton manufactures of this district are spinning of twist, and weaving of strong fustians, with other cotton goods.

General History of Saddleworth.

From the earliest period to the present time.

Saddleworth. The etymology of which as settled by dame Tradition, was taken from the word as a whole, without attempting a dissection of its parts. The *palsied dame* was convinced the whole valley passed by conveyance, and the amount was not paid *in money* for the purchase thereof, but by the *tender of a Saddle*, whether a *Hackney* or a *Pack Saddle* our antiquarian Grandame has not yet come to a proper conclusion.* Suppose however, (as younger people sometimes differ in opinion from old ones,) we divide the word into parts, Sad—del—worth. Sad, (etymology uncertain,) gloomy, dismal,—Del, [Belgic) a valley,—

* This etymology puts me in mind of an old woman who once asked me very seriously if I knew why Oldham took its name, as she was sure she did? I answered in the negative, expecting from my querist a most astonishing answer. "O (said she) but I'll explain it fully to you, a party of "*fine folks*" once called at B***y Bamford's public house, and asked the name of the town, she answered Oldham. Oh rejoined one of the party, I have heard that my great, great Grandfather, (Mr. Quiz) being on a hunting party once called in this town, and because they could only procure for them for dinner some rancied ham collop, he and the party christened it **OLDHAM.**"

Worth, (or Werth, Saxon,) part of a parish; or from Scaw—del—worth, the woody valley.

That it was formerly a tractless and gloomy forest, all antiquarians are agreed, and consequently its remote history must be also gloomy and obscure. It is probable (according to Whitaker,) that when the Romans conquered this island, they made a road from Mancunium, (modern Manchester,) to Cambodunum, (modern Slack,) in the county of York; premising thus, and supposing as is agreed by antiquaries in general, that the Romans always projected their roads in a direct manner, over hill and dale, it must certainly have passed through this district, and very near in the line of Castle Shaw, near Delph. On the conquest of the Romans, the conquered people, or ancient Britons, or Aborigines, inhabitants of the island, would probably retreat to the mountains of Wales, and a small party, (it may be conjectured,) retired into the forests and fastnesses of Saddleworth, and other remote and hilly regions, and gave names to the three streams, which yet retain their true and genuine British names. viz. the Tame, the Chaw, and the Diggle, " these (says the learned Whitaker of Holme,) are more remains of the original language, than in those parts where the general use of it was early superceded by the Saxon. The Diggle is evidently the same with the Douglas of Lower Lancashire, recored by *Nennius*, for one of the victories of Arthur, and with the Douglas of Scotland memorable for having given name to the most illustrious family in that kingdom. And it is not less evidently compounded of *Dhu-glas*, altro cæruleus. Drayton who is often learned, as well as accurate in epithets, calls the former "Swart Douglas." Tame, (vide supra,) is nothing more than the general appellation, *av* or *am*, with one of the prepositive letters. Chaw is the same, though it may be difficult to assign a meaning origin to the singular prefix. *Keg* seems to approximate nearer to it than any other word, and Kegaw would be gutter-aquæ." Of the language of the ancient Britons, there are few remains, but the above streams prove that this district was once inhabited by these ancients.

In the third volume of the memoirs of the Literary and Philosophical Society of Manchester, page 292, is the following essay, by Mr. Thomas Barritt, a late learned antiquary of Manchester. "About a mile westward of Saddleworth Church, in the county of York, is a high hill, which commands an extensive prospect over the adjacent country. The place is called by the neighbouring people POTS and PANS. Upon the summit are abundance of large craggy stones, (of that sort generally called Mill-stone Grit,) lying scattered up and down, which when viewed from the east look like the foundation or ruins of some stupendous fabric. One of these stones, or rather two of them joined together, is called the PANCAKE; it is of an irregular square form with obtuse angles, and hath upon its surface four basons hollowed in the stone, the largest being nearly in the centre, is capable of holding eight or ten gallons of water, some say more: whether these hollows be natural or artificial, is not known. This stone I measured and found to be about 76 feet in circumference. Another long uneven hole upon this stone, is called

c

Robin Hood's Bed. A little westward of this is another stone, about twenty feet in height, but much narrower at the top, from whence proceed irregular flutings or ridges down one side, of about two feet long, by some supposed to be the effect of time, and by others the workmanship of art. More westward, and nearer the valley of Greenfield, the ground is called Aldermans, and overlooks that valley, opposite to a large and high rock called Alphin. Upon the level of this ground is a fissure in the earth about twelve or fourteen yards long, each end terminating in a cavernous hole in the rock, one of which is capable of admitting dogs, foxes or sheep; the other large enough to receive men. Neither of these cavities has been thoroughly explored by any one, within my memory;* a person informed me he had gone into the larger with a light, but returned after having gone down a sloping descent of about sixty yards: Tradition says into the other hole once went a dog in full chase after a fox, but neither of them ever yet returned.

To a superficial observer unacquainted with ancient history, and busied only with the common occurrences of the present day, these rude remains may appear to be no more than the sport or chance of nature, thus left when the water of the General Deluge quitted its earthly seat, and fixed its residence in its proper bed. To guess at the transactions of remote ages, where we have no written authority, is, it must be owned, too often fallacious, and at best very uncertain, and some

---

* They have both been explored since, as vide hereafter.

whose inclinations or pursuits do not coincide with such researches, may slight those attempts which lead to actions as far back as "twice ten hundred years;" yet where we cannot attain complete knowledge, it is humbly presumed a probable conjecture may be admitted. Upon this conjecture we may go and say that situations like these, and stones like those we describe, have been made use of in the most ancient idolatry, and particularly by the Druids of this island, who as priests of its first inhabitants, performed the rites of their religion upon high grounds, as most suited to the solemnity of their worship; and as they might suppose the Deity to be more propitious when addressed from a lofty eminence, "they worshipped the whole expanse of heaven, and had open temples." Sacred History assures us this was the custom amongst idolatrous nations in the east. Now it may be allowed that the residence of a Druid thus elevated upon a mountain would the better command respect from a surrounding crowd, who had an opportunity for many miles round, of beholding the smoke ascend from a burning sacrifice. The stone called Pancake, (says he,) I shall venture to point out as an altar once used for sacrifice, for libations, for offering the fruits of the earth, for divination, by the entrails of beasts, the flight of birds, by water, and other methods, of which we are not now acquainted. Borlase, in his antiquities of Cornwall, gives us a very learned and accurate account of Druidical history, and describes these stones or karns with great minuteness, and whoever will take the trouble to read his work, may be thoroughly convinced that these stones in

Saddleworth, were originally for the same use as those he describes in Cornwall. In speaking of hollows or basons, (he says) "These basons are generally found on the highest hills, and on the most conspicuous karns; some are found sunk into thin flat stones, but they are oftener worked into more substantial and massy rocks." He seems not to allow of their being "designed for altars,* either of sacrifice, of libation, or holy fires," but I must say that the stone called Pancake might be accommodated to those purposes, with care. He thinks these basons wholly calculated for the Pagan superstitions of "lustration, and purifications by water." The purest of all water is that which comes from the heavens in snow, rain, or dew, and of this the ancients were not ignorant; and therefore no water seems to be more justly preferable in those sacred rites than this.

"It may with great probability be advanced, that so strict a sect as that of the Druids, could not be ignorant of so universal a custom, nor knowingly forbear to adopt so ancient and specious a rite for a part of their system: my opinion therefore is, that the Druids, as well as other priesthoods, had the rites of external purification, by washing and sprinklings, for this they had their holy water; and that this holy water was rain or snow, or probably both, and that these rock basons were vessels most ingeniously contrived to procure that holy water. They likewise had their waters of jealousy, as well as the Jews, and near the banks of the Rhine, use the water of that river to purge the suspected.

* Borlase does allow that ancient heathen priests did sacrifice upon rocks.

These basons are mostly placed above the reach of cattle, and frequently above the inspection of man." These long hollows, such as Robin Hood's Bed, upon the stone called Pancake, Barlase supposes " were to receive the bodies of men and children, for particular disorders, that by the healing virtues attributed to the god who inhabited the rock, they might be cured of their ailment; or by being prostrated on so holy a place, might be fitted for and consecrated to the service of the rock deity, for which they were intended." In confirmation of the above, a notion hath prevailed to the present, that the water of the bason in the centre of Pancake, will cure sore eyes, which superstition, I suppose, hath continued since the days of Druidism, and seems to establish the existence thereof, in this part of the country. The water in the rock basons might serve to mix with their misletoe, which was looked upon as a general antidote.

About half a mile north of Pancake, are several large stones piled upon each other, upon the highest of which is a hollow or bason, these are called STAPELEY STONES. What the word Stapeley may signify is uncertain; it may come from the Belgic word Stapel, a settled market: perhaps in this place necessary articles were sold to the Druids, and others who came to worship, the venders not being permitted to approach any nearer the sacred ground. Not far from this ground also was found the *Stone Celt*,* described by Mr. Whitaker, in his history of Manchester. The large upright stone,

* An instrument used by the Druids to cut off the misletoe.

about twenty feet in height, erected at some little distance from Pancake, I should suppose was the stone idol, once here worshipped; around it are many large stones, lying in all directions, as if tumbled one from off another. If it be admitted that this hill has been dedicated to heathen worship, the ground called Aldermans I should imagine to extend to the place where the idol once stood. The word Aldermans I suppose not to be its original name, but to have been afterwards given by the Saxons, signifying in their language the Elderman, or Old Man, from a rock idol, once worshipped here, by the Celtic Britons, the true name of which was unknown to the Saxons, as it is to us now living. So that upon the whole I should conclude that a rude stone pillar was once worshipped upon this hill, and that the stone called Pancake was the altar, and the stones now lying confusedly dispersed about, composed (though of rude materials,) once an heathen temple, which upon the prevalence of Christianity, and the rise of more enlightened times, was destroyed, nay, is even to this day wasting more and more.

At Mow Cop in Cheshire is a rude upright stone pillar, called the Old Man of Mow, and said by the country people to be an idol, once used for idolatrous worship, perhaps at the same time with this in Saddleworth. For a description of the subterraneous caverns before just mentioned at Alderman's, see the topographical notice of them under Aldermans. We shall now conclude our description of these remarkable antiquities, with a short account of the people who are supposed to have erected them.

The Druids were a body of men, who though generally considered as priests, acted in a civil as well as ecclesiastical capacity. The reason of their becoming possessed of secular as well as clerical authority, was owing to a notion being prevalent among the people, that none ought to submit to punishment for any crime whatever, but by divine authority, which authority was delegated to and lodged in the priest alone. Hence the Druids had an uncontrolled power over the minds and persons of the laity, exempted also from taxes, excused from military services, arbitrators in civil concerns, Judges in criminal matters, and public oracles of the community, it must be imagined hence, that their sentence was without appeal, indeed few dared dispute their infallibility. But if by chance an individual had so much temerity, he was punished by excommunication, so dreadful, as to be deemed more terrible than the most cruel death; from that moment he was considered as a person abandoned by God and man, universally hated and condemned, no one would associate with him; but he was suffered to drag through a miserable existence, till penury or sorrow snatched him from a world, in which he could neither obtain pity or relief. The Druids were of three classes, namely Druids properly so called, Bards, and Eubates or Vates. The first class presided over, and regulated all public affairs, both spiritual and temporal. The second class the Bards, were the national preceptors. It was also their business to compose songs, in commemoration of their heroes, and other eminent persons. Eubates, were skilled in physic, natural phylosophy, astronomy, magic, divination, augury, &c. They were under the direction of a principal, elected by themselves, and styled Arch Druid, whose authority extended so far as to call to account, and depose the secular prince whenever he thought proper. Their adoration, and religious ceremonies were performed in groves, consecrated to their deities. These groves were composed of and surrounded by, and fenced in with lofty oak trees, as they held sacred that towering monarch of the British plains. If any disturbance ever happened among the Druids, it was upon the death of their primate; when such earnest endeavourswere made to get appointed to that honorable and powerful office, that the freedom of election was frequently disturbed by appeals to the sword; upon all other occasions they acted with great justice, moderation, disinterestedness, and temperance, which at once secured and increased that respect the people naturally entertained for them. Their moral philosophy too hath been the admiration of after ages, and many of their maxims which stand in record, have met with the eulogium of the most celebrated and polished writers.

After the Druids in the order of time, we proceed to observe that the Romans left numerous remains of their castles, fortifications and roads in this country, one of which yet exists in Saddleworth, this is *Castleshaw*, which was probably only a small halting station of those conquerors, and its being about equal distance between their two more superior stations, (Manchester and Slack,) strengthens this opinion.

The Rev. John Watson, rector of Stockport, gives the following account of Castleshaw, " Castleshaw, in Saddleworth, was doubtless the first day's march of the Romans, from Manchester, and Slack the second, detachments also from this corps, might be left at this and other stations on this line of march, to keep the country in awe, and to prevent the communication from the southerly parts of England, with the troops at the Wall of Severus, being cut off or disturbed; they also did well to keep possession of these *" Castra pro unius diei itinere."* " *Camps for one day's march,*" that they might as soldiers on their motions, be sure of convenient lodging and other necessaries every night. And I am of opinion that these kind of garrisons seldom consisted of more than a centurion's command; both because the votive altars found in such are generally subscribed with the names and titles of these officers, and no other; and because this number of men seems quite sufficient for the purposes above mentioned; for in case of an attack, they could give notice to the neighbouring garrisons, by means of beacons, &c. and they were sure of immediate assistance. The general size of them shew that they were not intended for any greater number of troops, for the most part of them which I have seen do not exceed a hundred and twenty, or a hundred and thirty yards square, some not much more than a hundred."

A Roman altar has been discovered on the scite of Castlehill, it is of a square form with many plain ornaments, and the following inscription in front:

" FORTUNÆ
SACRUM
CAIUS ANTONIUS MODISTUS
CENTURIO
LEGIONIS SEXTÆ VICTRICUS
PIÆ FIDELIS
VOTUM SOLVIT
LUBENS
MERITO."

In English it will read thus :—" Caius Antonius Modistus, Centurion of the sixth, victorious, pious, and faithful legion, consecrated this altar to Fortune, and with pleasure discharged the vow which he owed."
The Centurion who commanded the Slack station when the above altar was erected, was one Caius Antonius Modistus, and I apprehend from the shape of the letters, and the triangular form of the punctuation, that it was set up soon after this place was garrisoned by a party of the sixth legion, which I take to be immediately after the arrival of Adrian, in the year of Christ 120, or thereabouts." The Rev. Mr. Whitaker speaking of the altar found at Castlehill, in Saddleworth, says, " Thus plainly are the remains evinced to be Roman, and thus clearly have we found what industry has vainly toiled for, and genius has ineffectually striven to discover, through the long extent of a century and a half, the real scite of *Campodunum*, and the Roman road to Manchester." Mr. Whitaker also supposes that it was in later times, a fortress of the provincial barons; but from what he can derive this singular conjecture, I know not.

It appears from the present elevation of the grounds, and the *Husteads*, and *Castle Hills*, that the extent of this Roman Castle occupied several statute acres; and round heads of the Britons have been dug up here, of the same kind, as those which have been discovered in the British barrows upon Salisbury Plain.

The Roman Iter, or Road to Slack, egressed out of Manchester on the east, and passed over Newton Heath, and through Failsworth, in a part of which are very visible remains of it; then crossing the Parochial Chapelry of Oldham, near or below Goldwick, and by Hey Chapel, whence it ascended to the summit of Austerlands, and entered the county of York, passing Knowl Hill, in Saddleworth, it crossed where the line of the Manchester and Huddersfield road now passes, within two furlongs of the Roman Station, at Castleshaw, leaving Marsden about a mile and a half to the south, it skirted Golcar Hill, and attained the plot of Campodunum, viz. Slack, or Almondbury. The word Castle Shaw, implies a Castle in a Wood, being once probably inclosed by a wood, and Castle Hill, the hill of the castle.

To the Romans succeeded the Saxons, who gave names to numerous places in this part of England, the word Grave is purely Saxon, whether single, as it sometimes occurs, or in the composition of other names, as it is now more frequently found, and denotes one of those deep and naked gullies, (and is used here as Goodgreave, Hollingreave,) which in the forests and on the sides of the hills, we see excavated by torrents, in the Schistus, and other minerals. Such are the remains of our Aboriginal language, which may be traced in local names, through this widely extended district, names which after the lapse of so many centuries, and the shock of so many revolutions, still subsist, and may probably continue as long as the objects they describe. It seems plain from many circumstances that the Danes, who were coeval with the Saxons, and (which the Saxon Chronicle confirms,) that under Canute, their king, they made a grand march through this parish. At page 147 we read that this Canute went against Uhtred, the Earl of Northumberland, through Buckinghamshire, Bedfordshire, Huntingdonshire, Lincolnshire, Nottinghamshire, and towards York; and the said Uhtred, being slain, he returned to the south, by the western coast, a different way from which he had gone before. And what way so likely as this, which the Romans had made from Manchester to York? It might then be in good repair, and if the king chose to march by the western coast, this was the next and best way; this march was in the year 1017. There are several very notable circumstances that confirm this opinion, that this Danish king did actually march along this road, such as Knott, (or Canute Lane, in Saddleworth,) and by the side of this Knott Hill, which is a remarkable round and copped hill, from the top of which this king is said to have harangued his army, (See Plot's Staffordshire,) there are other places on the direct line of the Roman road, which yield greater evidence to me of such a march, than any mentioned by Plot aforesaid, as from Saddleworth, the direct line for Street, in Failsworth, (where the Roman road is perfectly visible,) would lie through the higher part of the division of Knott Lanes, in Ashton-under-Lyne, even through Alt, (and there is now a tradition, that the army halted here,) and from Knott Hill, near Alt, he would be able again to have a full view of the marching army, and might harangue them again here. They passed hence to Knott Mill, near the Castle Field, Manchester, and thence to Knutsford, called by Camden *Canuti Vadum*.

Descending now to the period of time when the Norman Invader expelled the race of the Saxons, and by his prowess overwhelmned the nation and filled up the places of our Saxon ancestors, with an armed banditti of his followers, dividing the kingdom amongst those " he delighted to honour." This part of the country fell to the family of the Stapletons, the first of whom on record is Hugh de Stapleton ; William de Stapleton was his son and successor, about the 12th or beginning of the 13th century. But even in 1066, at the time of the conquest, Saddleworth was constituted a manor, and in consequence of this it would become more inhabited, and the land or rather the forests, better cultivated. The manor after this was sold by its primitive lords the Stapletons, to the Ramsdens ; from the Ramsdens it passed to Farrers, and the Holts, of Ashworth, the former of whom sold their share to the tenants.

Friar's Mere, in Saddleworth, was anciently Abbey Land, but at the dissolution of the monasteries, it was confiscated by Henry the eighth, and sold by that monarch to Arthur Ashton and Roger Gartside, for the sum of £624. which was paid to the crown by the aforesaid men, in the porch of the parochial chapel of Saddleworth, about the year 1543, there being then no public house in this district. In country places at that time it was usual to transact much public business in the vestries or porch of the respective place of worship, nearest to where the parties dwelt. Friar's Mere being thus once possessed by the Abbey of Whalley, is free from all tythes and tenths, and £2. 0 1d. is paid in lieu of these matters by the freeholders thereof, (formerly at the Castle,) but now at the Black Bull, in Preston, in the county of Lancaster. Perhaps a more remarkable instance of rise in the value of an estate cannot be produced than the following : on August 9th, 1654, William Farrer, Esq. of Ewood, near Halifax, purchased a share of the land of Saddleworth, from William Ramsden, Esq. of Longley Hall, for £2950, this in 1755 brought in a rent of £1500 per annum, to James Farrar, Esq. of Bamborough Grange; in 1780 he sold off estates to the value of £10,000, and by advancing the remainder kept up the same rent as before. At his death, in 1791, the rent was about £2000, much of it in leases for lives, and the estate being sold in small parcels to the occupiers and others, produced nearly £70,000, which added to the value of that sold before, makes a product of £80,000, from less than a £3000 original purchase, in the comparatively small space (considering the amazing advance in value,) of 137 years.. From the period of the reformation the tythes of the chapelry were paid to the Archbishops of Canterbury, until 1813, at which time an act of Parliament enabled the late Primate, Dr. Sutton, to sell them to the freeholders.

THE PAROCHIAL CHAPEL OF SADDLEWORTH.

There are not any imposing remains of architectural grandeur in Saddleworth. If we consider the early state of this district, and the early history of the people inhabiting it, the reason will appear obvious. Dwelling in a romantic, secluded, and at the period of the conquest, and long subsequent, an almost uncultivated tract of country, and for a succession of centuries, the vassals or tenants of opulent non-resident families, few of the superflous luxuries of the city, or the expensive ornaments of art could be expected to find their way into this remote part of Yorkshire. Although it has not been the lot of Christianity in this district, to dazzle the eye with the stately pillar and the glowing window, yet little doubt exists in the minds of antiquarians that Saddleworth was, in early times, eminent for its Temples of Religion. We may with as much certainty conclude that the surprising huge and craggy rocks on Aldermans, are Druidical remains, (so before remarked upon,) as that the celebrated rocks on Stonehenge, in Wiltshire, are of the same origin. Here then we conclude that the worshippers of the misletoe, celebrated their sacred rites and their rude and barbarous altars, are still silent though significant tokens of their religion. Thanks be to the All-wise disposer of all things, a blessed Redeemer appeared; preaching " glad tidings" of love and benevolence, and gloomy barbarism fled before the STAR OF THE

MAGI. This dark and forbidding era passed away, and the *Light from the East* beamed upon Saddleworth. By whom this light was first shed upon this district, is wrapt in impenetrable obscurity. We may adopt the language of the quaint though pious Dr. Fuller, the church historian, and say "the light of the WORD shone amongst us, but we know not who kindled it." In the course of time it would be found both expedient and necessary for a place of religious worship to be erected, for the accommodation of the inhabitants who had previously attended the service of the church at Rochdale, and perhaps Oldham. Since the reign of William the first, the whole district had been under the jurisdiction of the family of De Stapleton, ancestors of the present Sir Martin Stapylton, Bart, of Myton, in the West Riding of the county of York. Anxious for the moral and spiritual improvement of their tenantry, who alone occupied their manor of Saddleworth, and who had long found the inconvenience and almost impracticability of attending the public worship of God at places so far removed from them, we find by ancient charters or copies of them, still preserved in the Abbey of Whalley, in Lancashire,* that Hugo de Stapleton, then lord of this manor, requested permission from Hugh, earl of Chester, to build a chapel for the use of tenants. This application was conceded upon certain specified conditions, amongst which was that

* It will perhaps be correct to state that those charters with various grants, household books of expenditure, &c. connected with the Abbey, are carefully preserved in a chamber over the principal gateway leading to the Abbey, still remaining entire.

the chapel should be annexed to Whalley Abbey. Although Hugh de Stapleton appears to have succeeded in obtaining the grant from the Earl of Chester, subsequent documents shew that the chapel was not built by him, but by William de Stapleton, who was probably the son, or at least the successor of Hugh.

From a deficiency of chronological accuracy in the old deeds, we cannot ascertain the precise time when this parochial chapel was erected. Some modern topographers have asserted (whose accounts of Saddleworth seem inaccurate,) upon what authority we know not, that the building was erected " in the end of the 12th, or beginning of the 13th century." It appears from the plain, unquestionable authority of Dr. Whitaker, that the Abbey of Whalley was not built until Anno Domini, 1296. The endowments of Stanlaw, a small convent in Cheshire, belonging to the Lacys, were at that period transferred to Whalley, a branch of that family being probably settled there. This removal, by no means a common occurrence with our ancestors, arose from the bad scite of the religious house at Stanlaw. It was much exposed to frequent inundations, (then common in its immediate vicinage,) and other inclemencies of the seasons. This may account for the selection of the picturesque and secluded situation which the venerable ruins at Whalley now occupy. Hence the Chapel of Saddleworth being dependent on the Abbey of Whalley, could not be founded previous to the latter part of the 13th century.

An ancient charter proves that Geoffry, Dean of Whalley, and the Vicar of St. Cedde, or Chad, in Rochdale, with the sanction of the Patron of the Church, Roger de Lacy, gave license to Wm. de Stapleton, to cause divine offices to be performed in his chapel, at Saddleword. John, brother of the Dean, being a witness to the execution of the deed. This charter being granted at Whalley, must of necessity bear date subsequent to A. D. 1296. Notwithstanding that, the Chapel of Saddleworth was annexed to Whalley Abbey; it appears from another charter, that the tythes were not paid to it. " William de Stapleton swears upon the sacred relics, in the mother Church of Rochdale, St. Chad, to pay to the said mother church, all the tythes of the forest of Saddleword, and compel, (nomines sous,) his homagers to do the same, on which condition Roger de Lacy, and Geoffry, the Dean, licensed the chaplain, to celebrate in his chapel in Saddleword; to be presented to the parson of the mother church, and to swear canonical obedience,"—An oath always exacted of chaplains in ancient times. The date of this document is unknown, but as the parties appear to be the same as those concerned in the one just alluded to, we may infer that no very long space of time had elapsed. Robert another of the Stapletons, a near relative of William, grants, "for the use of a Chaplain, in the Chapel of Saddleword, thirteen acres of arable land, with a toft, on which to erect a competent manse, (parsonage,) for a Chaplain, pasture for ten cows, with their followers to three years old, eight oxen, and sixty sheep, with their lambs; salva venatione sua et avibus suis alias capientibus."* The manse, or " parsonage"

---

* This is a very early mention of hawking, which was revived as it is and has been called, from time immemorial, is still remaining, though, from having been an extensive range of building, or, as the donor of the glebe expresses it, "a competent manse," it has been suffered to dwindle into a cottage. Its situation, on the edge of the supposed Roman road which probably passed from the Roman station at Stockport, through Stayley-street, and so on to Castle Shaw, where it most likely formed a junction with that from Manchester to Slack, or Almondbury, a quarter of a mile west of the parochial Chapel of Saddleworth, is bleak and exposed, yet being on a fine eminence, it commands a pleasing prospect of the adjacent valley, and surrounding country for many miles. It is more than half a century since an Incumbent of Saddleworth regularly occupied the parsonage, and owing to its present dilapidated state, it is not calculated for the residence of a minister.

Lastly by another charter, also without date, a composition is made between the inhabitants of this district, and the Abbot and Convent of Stanlaw, (but who must then have been removed to Whalley,) by which it was agreed, that the former shall repair the body of their chapel, the enclosure of the yard, with the tower, and find bells for the same; and the latter shall repair the chancel of the chapel, and find books, and vestments.*

in Europe, about the date of this charter, by the Emperor Frederick Barbarossa, who died, A. D. 1189.

* There is in possession of R. H. Beaumont, of Whitley, Esq. a charter by which Robert de Stapleton, (probably the same as before mentioned,) grants "To God, the blessed Virgin, and Saints, and to James of Kirklees, eight acres in Saddleworth, housebote and haybote."

At the dissolution of the larger religious houses, by Henry the Eighth, in 1536, the Chapel of Saddleworth, from having been long dependent on Whalley, was annexed to the parish Church of Rochdale, (being the nearest parish and possessions of Whalley, adjoining to the forest of Saddleworth,) and the appointment of the minister was vested in the Vicar for the time being. The Vicar of Rochdale has supreme ecclesiastical jurisdiction throughout the district of Saddleworth, although the patronage is unimportant.

In 1661, Ralph Wood, the then Incumbent of Saddleworth, resigned his living rather than take the oath of conformity. In the latter part of the seventeenth century, there was a very distinguished minister here of the name of *Lees*, who died universally regretted, in 1721. Several anecdotes of him are still remembered, which tend to shew that he was a man of decided piety, and firmness of purpose.

The following are the names of the Incumbents of Saddleworth, during the last 140 years.

  1st. The Rev. Edward Lees, (aforesaid.)
  2nd. The Rev. John Higginbottom, M. A.
  3rd. The Rev. Richard Podmore, LLB.
  4th. The Rev. Edward Taylor,
  5th. The present Incumbent,

Viz. the Rev. Charles Zouch, M. A. who was appointed to the living in 1791, by Dr. Drake, the then Vicar of Rochdale. The present worthy officiating curate is the Rev. F. R. Raines.

The Chapel of Saddleworth being built while the country was in a sterile and rude state, and solely for the use of the tenantry, we are not at all surprised to find in it a deficiency of architectural skill and ornament. There is none of the rich and sumptuous tracery, or the gorgeous fretted work of that stately pile,* the pride and boast of this extensive county.

Here are none of the enshrined saints and martyrs, or the splendidly decorated tombs, that adorned some of the ancient churches, here are none of the glowing tints of Titian, the lively figures of Raphael, or the soft sweetness of Dominichino; we may however observe, that by some means or other, a barbarous daub, by an ignorant Tyro, has found its way into this parochial place of worship, and remains an offensive monument of the bad taste which placed it in its present situation. Tne subject is said to be Daniel in the Lion's Den; here are no "long drawn aisles,"—no "fretted vaults," "no storied urn,"—no "animated bust;" yet there is the humble simplicity of a pure and unadulterated taste, mingled with all the gloomy solemnity which so well befits the Temple of the Living GOD. Externally, the structure is a dark and heavy building. Its situation is bleak, about half a mile to the east of Saddleworth Fold, and it is not (whatever it may have been in former days,) protected from the "peltings of the pitiless storm," either by the sheltering branches of the gloomy elm, or the sacred yew. The parochial Chapel appears to have undergone many alterations and repairs at various periods. As the population increased, a deficiency of room in the interior of the structure would be experienced, to remedy which the south

* York Minster.

gallery would probably be the first that was erected, and this may account for the second tier of windows, in the front of the fabric. When this addition was made is to me unknown, but it would be subsequent to the Reformation.

After times found it requisite to extend the gallery round the whole of the interior, and the want of accommodation was found to be so urgent, that about the latter part of the seventeenth or the beginning of the eighteenth century, a second gallery was raised over the south one, and part of it was appropriated for the use of the regular singers then belonging to this place. The large and spacious western Gallery was built by a Mr. Kenworthy, "at his own sole expence," and the date of the erection of which is 1711. Thus the interior though neat, comfortable and plain, with a good middle and two side aisles, chancel, baptistry, and other conveniences, is heavy and unimposing in its appearance. In 1746, the old steeple was found to be in an insecure state, and was consequently taken down. It would be difficult to arrange the present steeple under any given order of architecture, and we may safely say, without incurring the censure of any living individual, that it reflects but little credit upon the taste of the designer. It may however have been the wish of the architect that it should synchronize with the body part of the structure, which we must bear in mind was erected not for the ostentatious display of the achievements of art, but for the more praise-worthy purpose of utility.

In 1781 a faculty was obtained to place six bells in the tower of this parochial chapel. This fine peal, the only one in Saddleworth, is justly admired for its melody and sweetness. In 1788, a good toned organ was presented to this parochial chapel, by the munificence of the principal inhabitants. Saddleworth has long been celebrated for its musical amateurs, and has produced some first rate public performers, amongst whom we name Miss Harrop, afterwards Mrs. Bates, the wife of Josiah Bates, Esq. of London.

The old oak seats, or as they are commonly called sittings, which had been in the body part of the church probably from its first foundation, were in 1825, at the suggestion of Bishop Law, completely removed, and new pews substituted in their place. All these are free to the inhabitants. The gallery pews belong to the land owners and householders of the parish. At the same time the aisles were neatly flagged, which previously had been of mud only.

During these improvements, the workmen in excavating the foundation for a flight of steps leading to the west gallery, hit upon a stone bason or trough, of considerable dimensions, but being ignorant of the nature of the relic, and deeming it in the first instance an ordinary stone, with the most reprehensible ferocity they broke it into numerous fragments, before it could meet the scrutinizing and vigilant eye of the antiquarian. It appears to have been an antique font or bason, for the reception of holy water. A remnant six or eight inches in length, and half that breadth, rudely carved, was subsequently placed on the top of the porch, but it is too minute to lead to any probable conjecture respecting the original use or design of the vessel, than the one aforenamed, which is suggested by a traditional description of the relic. Owing to the amazing increase of population during the last century, and the long use which had been made of the old church yard, it was found necessary to purchase an additional piece of ground for the reception of the inmates of mortality. The consecration of the same took place in 1824. On a grave stone in Saddleworth church yard, is the following inscription :

"M. S.
Ralph, son of Thomas Hawkyard, of Tame Water, Chapman, who for the propagation of Useful Learning, and the reformation of manners in this parish, left £200 absolute, and £110 more if his brother should die a minor and his sister childless, Obiit, Junii 19th, An. Dom. 1729. Ætatis 39.

> Be all his gifts improv'd ;
> Fresh be his name,
> While schools can last,
> Or goodness merit fame.

Also William Hawkyard, of Bridgehouse, who departed this life September 6th, 1776, in the 58th year of his age.

With a portion of this bequest the free school at Dobcross was built, where the English language and the rudiments of a common education, are now taught free of expence, to a limited number of poor children.

The following curious epitaph to the old sexton of Saddleworth appears, wrote (I suppose,) by Mr. Bottomley, the author of Greenfield, a poem, as it appears among his papers:

> Thrice sixteen years, extremely well
> He bore the bier and toll'd the bell,
> And cheerfully discharg'd his trust,
> In "earth to earth," and "dust to dust;"
> Let none lament, tho' life is spent,
> The *grave* is still his element;
> His old friend Death knew 'twas his sphere,
> So kindly laid the sexton here.

The church is in the central part of the parochial chapelry, and the ancient Roman road from Castleshaw, and thence to Stockport, passes close by it, though modern improvements have rendered its situation singular, and perhaps inconvenient. The church of Saddleworth, like most parochial chapels, is meanly endowed. The small quantity of land given by Robert de Stapleton, is the principal source of the Incumbent's emolument, which has recently been partially augmented by a grant from "Queen Anne's Bounty." At the enclosure some moor land was awarded to the church, but it has not been cultivated. From the period of the reformation the tithes of the chapelry were paid to the Archbishops of Canterbury, until 1813, at which time an Act of Parliament enabled the late primate, Dr. Sutton, to sell them to the freeholders.

The privilege of marrying is confined exclusively to the church, and the occupiers of pews are alone permitted to inter in the episcopal chapels. This bar however is not regarded by the inhabitants of Saddleworth, for the children of Israel have not a more ardent desire to be buried in the valley of Jehosophat, than the natives of this district have for their dust to mingle with that earth, which long acquaintance has rendered familiar to them, and which time has rendered sacred. There are indeed few churches to be found more enthusiastically venerated by their respective attendants than Saddleworth. For in the revolution of many centuries the only church frequented by their ancestors,—themselves educated in the liberal tenets of pure and apostolical religion,—and with each returning Sabbath visiting the ground where the peaceful ashes of their forefathers repose,—need we wonder that the parish church, the only antient public establishment in the district, should be regarded with feelings approaching almost to superstitious reverence? Such sentiments are laudible,—such feelings are honourable,—may they never be repressed.

There are two *Sunday Schools* connected with the church, one situated at *Diggle Bridge*, called *Kiln Green School*, containing in March 27th, 1828, 255 scholars; another at *Boarshurst*, where 200 children received instruction, according to the last return made as before stated. There are also several other considerable Sunday Schools in the parish of Saddleworth, one at *Warmton*, where 274 Scholars attended at the said date; one at *Castleshaw*, where 163 Scholars receive instruction every Sabbath, and another at *Denshaw*, where an equal number assemble for similar improvements. Total number of Scholars attending the different Sunday Schools in Saddleworth, is 1055.

TOPOGRAPHICAL DESCRIPTION

OF

SADDLEWORTH.

UPPER MILL, nearly a mile west of the church, is now becoming the first village in Saddleworth, and is eminently calculated so to be, from its local situation for trade, and many other advantages. The Huddersfield Canal passes through the village. The excellence also of the public road from Leeds to Manchester, with the intended improvements, is very likely to render this place a great thoroughfare between those very large and important towns. The houses are regularly built, the main thoroughfare through the place is also very spacious, and the whole displays an elegance of appearance that no other village of the district can at present boast. And I think we may anticipate that the period is not far distant, when this village may vie, through its local situation and numerous advantages, as before recited, with any other place in Saddleworth, both as regards its population and also its trade.

Here are two Methodists' Meeting Houses, at each termination of the village. The more elegant one is situate on your entrance from Huddersfield; this is a stone erection, with a burial ground attached. It was erected in 1811. The other called *Ebenezer*, being the older one, stands at the opposite and southern extremity of the place, on the road leading to Oldham, Ashton-under-Lyne, &c. and was erected in 1807.—To each of these places of worship, a Sunday School is annexed.

A fair is held at Upper Mill, on the 13th of June, annually, for cattle, pedlary, &c. The woollen manufacture is carried on here very extensively, in all its various branches. Under these peculiar local advantages, with its proximity to the canal aforesaid, and also its excellent roads, it is very likely to increase both in wealth and population. Its situation is low and warm, being sheltered by opposite hills, in a great degree, from the terrific winter blast, that howls over the mountainous regions of this district. This village is situate about half a mile below Dobcross, in a valley, and contains several elegant houses, a number of respectable shops, and three public houses, for the accommodation of travellers, particularly the *Commercial Inn*, where the magistrates of the district hold a justice meeting for the settling of the public business, alternately here, and also at Dobcross. It is distant five miles east of Oldham, thirteen and a half miles south west of Huddersfield, six miles north north east of Ashton-under-Lyne, and about two miles to the south of Delph, and twelve miles east from Manchester.

I now commence the general description of Saddleworth, which chiefly consists of numerous hamlets and small villages, scattered over the whole extent of the vallies of this district, and also on the declivities of the hills. Saddleworth, a century ago, was a well wooded country, the remains of the ancient forest, and was then probably more agreeable to the eye of a romantic traveller, than its appearance now exhibits. Its gently undulating vallies, its lofty and umbrageous mountains, its silvery Tame, its chrystal Diggle, and its lucid Chaw, though the two latter are as yet unrecorded by the *Bard of the Mountains*. All these combined together must have rendered it as interesting, sublime, and magnificent as the far famed scenery of Derbyshire.

Entering Saddleworth, above Lees, part of which is in the parish of Ashton-under-Lyne, and part now in Oldham, and another part also in the chapelry we are now attempting to describe, we advance to *Spring Head*, now become a small village, through the introduction of the woollen and cotton manufactures, which flourish here : it is agreeably situated on the road from Oldham to Upper Mill, about two and a half miles east of the former place, and about the like distance west from the latter. Here is a chapel of the Universalists, with a very neat cemetery adjoining. It is a handsome stone erection. A Sunday School belonging to the same, is situate opposite thereto.

A short distance on the left, as we ascend towards Lidgate, is *Walkers*, and also the elegant house of John Radcliffe, Esq. in a warm secluded valley, or rather declivity, called *Stone Breaks*, with a cluster of dwellings surrounding the same.

A short distance from this road, ascending towards Lydgate, you psss an ancient though small village, called *Thornley*, (i. e. the field of thorns.) I remarked an ancient dwelling here, on which are these initials: I. H. 1648. It is pleasantly seated in the midst of rich meadow land.

Ascending the steep hill above, and journeying east, we reach *Lydgate*, a small village on the road from Newhouses to Mossley; here is a Chapel of Ease of the Establishment, dedicated to St. Anne. It stands on the top of a bleak hill, it is a stone fabric, with a burial ground attached thereto, which was consecrated and the chapel erected in 1787, by Dr. Cleaver, Bishop of Chester. It is ornamented with a cupola. The present worthy minister is the Rev. Herbert Allken.

Lydgate being situated on a high and cold elevation, as aforesaid, enjoys one of the most extensive views in the parish; to the east is seen the bold and romantic cliffs, and broken precipices of Greenfield, whose picturesque scenery is fully displayed and meets our astonished view, while the wandering Tame in all his silvery mazes and strange meanderings, through the capacious and beauteous valley, discloses itself, pouring along its waters below the mountainous regions of Stealey, and the frowning mound-topped Buckton. To the west a perfect contrast presents itself, a rich, flourishing and fertile country, "far as the eye can reach," enclosed in on the south west by the Cambrian hills, and on the direct point west, by the bluey ridge of Horwich, on the north by the lofty Pendle, and his lesser compeer the nodding Tor. In the distance appears the long-stretched vapour ascending from the great and populous *Mancunium*, (Manchester,) the more distant and lighter discoloured clouds of smoke that mark out Stokeport, (Stockport,) and Boltonia, (Bolton,) with Oldham and Ashton-under-Lyne in the foreground, full in our view.

The cotton and woollen manufactures employ the inhabitants of the village, several cotton mills being in and near it. Lydgate is about one mile and three quarters from Upper Mill.

In this vicinity is the ancient mansion of *Grotton Head*, long the residence of the family of the Shaws. A short distance to the south lies *Quick*, and *Quick Edge*, which united may be considered as a small village.

Quick lies on the steep side of an elevated ridge of land, called *Quick Edge*, from whence is a most delightful view of the valley, and the romantic termination thereof in the rocky cliffs of Greenfield which are here exhibited full to our view. Here are situate several genteel habitations, particularly Messrs. Hilton's and Kenworthy's.

About half a mile to the south, in the vicinity of the village of Mossley, is situate *Carr Hill*, a hamlet consisting of a number of irregularly built dwellings, and the genteel houses of Messrs. Buckleys, and near thereto the ancient habitation called *Mossley Hall*, once the residence of a family of the local name, and after them possessed by the Kenworthys.

Brookbottom, a few paces nearer to, and almost adjoining the village of Mossley, has very much increased of late, and may now rank as one of the principal villages of Saddleworth; here are several large cotton mills, and numerous ranges of cottages inhabited chiefly by the mechanics, and other people employed in these mills. It is distant about three miles, S. S. W. of Upper Mill. A fair was formerly held at Brookbottom, which has been discontinued about eighty years.

Retracing back our steps about one mile and a half, in the direction of Upper Mill, we come to the elegant mansion of *Grove*, situated on the ascent of an agreeable eminence, embosomed in shades, and a little above there stands the neat looking village of *Grass Croft*, consisting of a number of stone habitations, built in an irregular manner, on the declivity of that hill on which Lydgate aforenamed stands. Here are several woollen manufactories, and the elegant mansions attached to them have a pleasing appearance.

Descending herefrom we come to *Clough*, or *Grass Croft Clough*, a retired hamlet. Still further at the junction of the Mossley and Oldham roads, leading to Upper Mill, lies *Shaw Hall*, on the steep and wooded side of a hill, called *Warmton*, which forms a prominent object to the encircling valleys, and from its summit is an extensive prospect of all the surrounding country.

"Solemnly vast. The trees of various shade,
Scene behind scene, with fair delusive pomp,
Enrich the prospect."

Dyer.

Descending into the rich and capacious valley, on the eastern side of Warmton, we cross the river Tame, and are gratified with a diversified landscape, the heights of Warmton on one side, soaring aloft in majestic form, opposed by the still more lofty mountains of Alder and Alphin, closed by Dove Stone Cliffs to the east, form in their united embrace the beautiful valley of Greenfield.

> "See Greenfield opens to the wondering eye,
> With a grand picture of antiquity!
> Hills thrown on hills, and rocks on rocks are pil'd,
> In hoary grandeur through this rural wild.
> *Bottomley's Greenfield, a Poem.*

The waters of the Chaw, which wind their way through this delightful vale, add an additional charm to the beauties that are here disclosed.

> "From the moist meadow to the withered hill,
> Led by the breeze, the vivid verdure runs,
> And swells, and deepens to the cherish'd eye.
> The hawthorn whitens; and the juicy groves,
> Put forth their buds, unfolding by degrees,
> Till the whole leafy forest stands display'd
> In full luxuriance to the sighing gales;
> Where the "kine" rustle thro' the twining brake,
> And the birds sing, concealed."
> *Thomson.*

Description and language though of the most luxuriant kind, possess not the powers of fully displaying the picturesque scenery which presents itself on approaching nearer to Greenfield, the most romantic part of which is seen on approaching the *Mill.* The summits of the hills on each side stretch into extensive moorlands, while at their feet is disclosed a luxuriance of highly cultivated lands.

Leaving French Mill, we pass two neat mansions called *Green Bridge* and *Oak View,* encircled by sylvan scenery, of the most desirable kind; and near to these places lies the ancient mansion named *Foul Rakes,* surrounded by lofty and venerable oaks, above which is a hamlet denominated *Kinders;* a short distance from hence lies the detached hamlet of *Boar's Hurst,* (or the Wood of the Boar,) it is situate about one mile S. E. of Upper Mill, here is a School used both as a Day and Sunday School.

Holly Ville, the beautiful mansion of James Buckley, Esq. is seated on the declivity of Aldermans, overlooking the valley of Greenfield, and at a short distance from Boar's Hurst, this is perhaps the most elegant mansion in the chapelry; in front of the mansion is an elegant portico, of free stone, corresponding with the majestic appearance of the house, which is situated amongst extensive plantations of perennials, the sloping lawns, the flowery walks, and the gloomy though pleasing shades, inspire the mind to contemplation. The prospect from hence is grand, the rugged mountain of Aldermans impending above in hoary grandeur, with the woody expanse of Greenfield, and the opposite barren elevations, form an extremely grand contrast, to the rich, delightful, and varied scenery around the house, below which the wanderings of the Tame, and the Chaw shed a radiance on the beautiful view exhibited herefrom.

> How still the scene, how fair, how grand!
> The light so soft, the shades so deep!
> O! such a scene might raise the heart,
> Transport to heaven the soul of joy!

The road to Greenfield leaves that to Huddersfield a little below Holly Ville, and winds its way through plantations of trees, along the banks of the meandering stream of the Chaw, till we come to a substantial wooden bridge at the foot of lofty Aldermans; here that beautiful scene opens, where is disclosed the elegant house, and nearly adjoining the large woollen manufactory of Mr. Bottomley's, called *Greenfield Mill*, and all the bold and romantic scenery surrounding the place, bursts at once upon the admiring and astonished eye of the beholder. On the declivity of Aldermans are very extensive plantations, the level plain intervening betwixt here and the foot of Alphin, is laid out in pleasing walks. The scene here is almost Elysian, the hoary grandeur of the almost perpendicular rocks of Dove Stone, immediately in front, with the semicircular ridge of Alphin, all combine to render Greenfield as romantic perhaps as any part of Derbyshire; and the pride and boast of the inhabitants of the chapelry.

The Mill aforesaid, (occupied at present by Mr. James Bottomley,) is one of the largest mills in Saddleworth, and here that business is carried on very extensively.

"The shelter'd vales are interspers'd with woods,
For ever green and sweet translucent floods;
While chrystal springs from mossy grottos stray,
And on their margin sportive lambkins play."
Bottomley.

And again his muse, descriptive of Dove Stone, thus begins:

But if great DOVE STONE'S lofty top we gain,
Impending dreadful o'er the sylvan plain,
Charm'd with new wonders, raptur'd as we rise,
Climes far remote the wand'ring eye descries;
Woods, plains, and spires, and many a distant town,
Fair England's pride, the circling landscape crown.
Down *Dove Stone Dean*, beneath the mountain's brow,
Of healing power, the mineral waters flow;
Where nymphs and swains at evening hour repair
From distant plains, to breathe the purer air."
Ibid.

Ascending the hill of Alderman, above Greenfield, another grand and sublime view opens again to sight, that singularly elevated hill, with the massy detached rocks on the summit, and the woody reclining valley below, are truly admirable. In these mountainous regions, are two deep and awful precipices, composed of huge rock stone, named Dove and *Raven Stones*, the latter of which appears more tremendous of the two, but from the top of which a person descended by means of a rope, for the purpose of taking a young eagle's nest, in which project he succeeded, (though on viewing it, one shudders at the idea of such a descent,) and to be thus suspended over such a tremendous precipice.

None but those who have visited these scenes of nature, can conceive what pleasure they impart to enquiring minds. The rocks of Raven Stone are about two miles above Greenfield, and Dove Stones about one. In these romantic glens, and near to Raven Stone, is a noted public house, called by the inhabitants of the surrounding country "Bill o' Jacks," which in the summer season is much frequented by numerous parties, who are admirers of the romantic beauties of the place; or others who repair here with line or gun to amuse themselves, will often stray so far up this sequestered valley, and the youngsters of the neighbourhood, to gather bilberries, frequently come here.

> For now with wicker baskets neat,
>   Behold the youthful train,
> With mirthful voice, the sheep tracks beat;
>   O'er hill, and vale, and plain;
> All on the moorlands spread the swains,
>   And many a lovely she,
> And there in song and cheerful strains,
>   They pick the bilberry.

The prospects we enjoy from these hills, with the purity of the air, are great incentives, and often induce a visit to these secluded regions, and may with great propriety be said amply to repay the toil attendant thereon, to any inquisitive mind.

On the summit of the hill of Aldermans, "are those dreary chasms, called by the inhabitants *Fairy Holes*, and the different opinions of persons who have frequented the place, determined me (says Mr. Robinson,) to have an excursion to those subterraneous passages.— The weather being favourable, I set out together with a few friends, towards the latter end of June, being provided with lights and other things necessary for the journey, we ascended the hill called Aldermans. The situation of the place is little more than one mile distant from the parochial chapel of Saddleworth, (in a south east direction,) about fifty yards from the summit of the rock on the top of the hill, rather north, descending a few yards. We lighted our candles, it being quite calm: the entrance for about six or seven yards, is rather straight, with a vaulted roof called Piccadilly, until it gives a turn or winding, assuming the name of Doby Street, when it descends almost perpendicular for a considerable length; when we arrived at the bottom, we come to a broad passage which is called Cupid's Alley; it has two passages, one to the right and the other to the left, the former not extending very far. Proceeding to reconnoitre the other, we came to a corner that was rather dangerous.

> A deeper horror seiz'd the mind,
> When from this rock you look behind,
> Your beating heart its breast repels,
> And dreads the danger of these cells.

At this corner there are projecting rocks, about twelve feet high, and rather difficult of ascent; arriving at the top we found the road very good for a considerable way, then descending and turning back to the right, under a large heap of rocks, to the same place where we ascended the rocks, at the corner the passage became rather straight for some yards, then opening to a broad deep dreary chasm, which is called the Devil's Cellar.—

> Should Pluto from his region roam,
> Within this cell he'd find a home,
> With ugliness it seem'd adorn'd,
> And perfect blackness like him form'd.

The rocks on both sides are almost perpendicular, and nearly parallel to each other: we proceeded down the cavern until we came to the bottom, and finding the rocks lay upon the shoal, which was a plain indication that we were at the bottom of the subterraneous vault; then returning back, we measured the road, and taking the angles, the result was, from the bottom to the top 45 yards, and about thirty yards perpendicular from the surface of the earth, or the first entrance of the cavern."

From this cavern the poet of Greenfield says, the explorer will return,

> And eager back the winding path will tread;
> Heav'ns! what transition then again to rise
> From realms of death, and view the radiant skies.

This place has been again recently visited by Mr. J. Platt, Schoolmaster, of Boarshaw School, and Mr. William Nicholson, of Lees, and they prove that Mr. Robinson's plan of the cavern was rather erroneous, inasmuch as that Coney Street and St. John's Street, extend to the *right* and not to the *left*, as shewn by Mr. Robinson's plan. They have also added other names to several short passages unnoticed by Mr. Robinson.

The following (according to their plan,) is an estimate of the length of the different passages and intricacies of the cavern :—Piccadilly, 7 yards; Queen Mab's Bedchamber, 3 yards; Doby Street 6 yards; Cupid's Alley, 6 yards; Nicholson's Gallery, $8\frac{1}{2}$ yards; Fox's Kennel, (not explored by Mr. Robinson,) 4 yards; George Street to Falstaff's Corner, $9\frac{1}{2}$ yards; Halliwell Street, $9\frac{1}{2}$ yards; Broadbent's Passage, 10 yards; the Devil's Cellar or Confusion Street, 8 yards; Nox's retreat, (or Short Street,) 2 yards; Coney Street to Elliot's Treasury, 9 yards; St. John's Street, 6 yards, and Beelzebub's Pantry, (not explored by Robinson,) $3\frac{1}{2}$ yards.

There is also another cavern of larger dimensions, according to the account of the late explorers, which lies very near the other, but of which they have no particular account or plan, and therefore I decline giving any further particulars thereof than this, (not having had the pleasure of visiting the same,) but which I have been informed was so capacious, as to be capable of containing a vast number of persons at the same time; the interior thereof (Mr. Platt said,) was very lofty, and the roof seemed to have been worked or formed by art. If such be the case, it tempts one to suppose it might be a Druidical or other retreat, for one must suppose, that though it is agreed by all historians and antiquarians, that they worshipped on the tops of the highest hills, or in the deep recesses of the lowest vallies, and ever in the open face of day, and "that the canopy of heaven alone was their covering," yet they must have some retreat, some shelter from the inclemency of the weather, or the prowling incursions of the beasts of the forest, they would therefore naturally shelter in caves, and subterraneous places in the earth.

Descending from these heights, we come to the ancient hamlet of *Tunstead*, agreeably situated amongst some rich pasture ground, which though surrounded by fences of stone, (which are the general mode of inclosing the lands here,) render it upon the whole, not at all an unpleasant situation. On an Out-building at this place are remaining (in 1828,) these initials, L. W. 1611, this must be one of the most ancient records on any common inhabited or uninhabited house in the Chapelry.

A little below Tunstead lie several neat habitations, called *Far Lane*, in one of which that seems to bear marks of high antiquity, resides a Mr. Robert Shaw. Nearer Upper Mill is a small place named Goburn Clough; and still further advancing nearer the Church, is the pleasant cluster of habitations called *Cross*.

Not far distant from the last mentioned place, stands the well-built mansion of *Heath Fields*, surrounded by some agreeable plantations; on the eminence above here lies the compactly built village of *Saddleworth Fold*, commanding a pleasing prospect of the encircling valley.

A little above you arrive at the venerable Parochial Chapel of Saddleworth, and in its immediate vicinity are two public houses, one of which the Cross Keys, was kept for several ages by the family of the Bottomleys, of whom was the poet Bottomley, the author of Greenfield.

About half a mile to the northward, lies the very detached and scattered hamlet of *Hollin Grove*, or *Greave*, (anciently so,) in which are situate several respectable houses; and in its neighbourhood lie also *Hollins*, and *Fearnlee*, two small places, all of which places are about one and a half miles N. E. of Upper Mill.

In a valley formed by the hilly regions called *Harrop Edge*, on the west, *Stand Edge*, (i. e. Stoney Edge,) on the north, and the extended ridge of Alderman, on the south east, stands the little village of *Diggle Bridge*, consisting of a few cottages, and a Sunday School, on the banks of the Huddersfield Canal, in a deep and almost secluded valley, nearly encircled by moorlands, two miles east of Upper Mill. A little above Diggle Bridge the aforesaid Canal makes its ingress into the celebrated tunnel before remarked upon in a former part of this work.

A small remove from hence in a north easterly direction, on rather a small ascent, lie several woollen mills, called *Court*, and on an eminence above which are a number of habitations, bearing the name of *Warwick Hill*, and *Foot*, from hence we have a fine prospect of the valley, generally denominated Harrop Dale, which extends to Wool Road in the distance.

"Here down this dale the Diggle's winding brook
Falls hoarse, from steep to steep. Come ye array'd
Fit for the thickets, and the tangling shrub,
For you, ye moorland maids, their latest song
The woodlands raise; the clustering nuts for you
The lover finds, amid the secret shade,
And, where they burnish on the topmost bough,
With active vigour crushes down the tree,
Or shakes them ripe from the resigning husk;
A glossy shower, and of an ardent brown."

Altered from Thomson.

Leaving Warwick hill, we cross the Huddersfield Road, and ascend to *Carr*, a few cottages built on the steep side of a hill. In the vicinity of the two before mentioned places is *Running Hill Head*, a small hamlet, with the Saddleworth *Work House* near the same.

At the very extremity of the valley of Harrop Dale stands a collection of houses, denominated *Black Hey Nook*, distant from Dobcross about two miles, and nearly three miles north of Upper Mill, on the Oldham and Huddersfield Road.

From the top of Harrop Edge, the prospect of the surrounding hills is very bold and impressive; the village of Wool Road appears from hence, as if quite secluded and shut up by the mountain scenery.

On the main road from Upper Mill to Huddersfield stands the small hamlet of *Weakey*, consisting of a public house, and a few cottages.

Nearer Wool Road lies *Marslands*, a small place on an agreeable elevation, overlooking the Diggle, which flows below.

Still further we come to the pleasant and improving village of *Wool Road*, situated at the junction of the Dobcross road, with that from Upper Mill to Huddersfield, along which it is built in the form of a street, containing several neat habitations, also an Inn, with a large and commodious canal warehouse, situate about half a mile above Upper Mill, and at a similar distance from Dobcross.

On an eminence below Wool Road stands the rural and picturesque habitation, called *Brown Hill*, with some beautiful gardens in front. The valley here is thickly studded with young trees, which impending over the banks of the murmuring Tame, and the smooth unruffled stream of the canal, form altogether a pleasant sylvanic scene.

Crossing the canal a little above, and ascending a steep hill we enter the village of DOBCROSS, one of the principal in the district, as respects the population; it consists of a steep street of cottages, erected on the side of a hill, and on the road from Wall Hill to Wool Road, five miles E. S. E. of Oldham, six and a half miles N. N. E. of Ashton-under-Lyne, thirteen and a half miles S. W. of Huddersfield, twelve miles E. N. E. of Manchester, one and a half miles S. S. E. of Delph, and half a mile north of Upper Mill. Dobcross was formerly called Woods; tradition says that the first habitation here, of any consequence, was inhabited by a person of the name of Wood, from whom it probably obtained the name of Woods, and some old people still denominate the place Woods. Nearly in the centre of the village stands an *Episcopal Chapel*, dedicated to the Holy Trinity; it is a plain yet handsome fabric of stone, graced by a small cupola of wood, the chapel is surrounded by a burial ground, containing several tombs, and other memorials respecting the defunct reposers underneath. This place of worship was erected for the use of the inhabitants, in the year 1787, and consecrated by Dr. Cleaver, the then Bishop of Chester, in the same year. The interior contains a gallery, in which is placed a small organ, and the whole of the interior is neatly pewed. The cemetery is overshadowed by some trees, which seem suited to the solemnity of such a place, where repose the respected ashes of our progenitors, or those we loved. The present curate is the Rev. Thomas Sturges Mills.

> Here cold in death, beneath their shade,
> Sleeps Mary dear, the moorland maid!
> Death O my soul! the worm now preys,
> On whom, the lover could for ever gaze!
> Yet Death accurs'd destroyer of our race,
> And thee vile worm, that spoil'st the finest face,
> I scorn ye both—for mem'ry with each tear,
> Brings back her angel form—I have her here.

The *Free School*, at Dobcross, appears to have been founded with a portion of the bequest of Ralph Hawkyard, of Tame Water, where the English language and the rudiments of a common education, are now taught free of expence, to a limited number of poor children.

In Dobcross are several woollen mills, and likewise some genteel houses. There is here a post office, which has long been established. The present post master is Mr. John Wrigley.

There are also two banks.

The place is well accommodated with respectable shops, and four public houses.

At the Swan Inn, the magistrates for the division of Saddleworth (viz. James Buckley, Esq. and the Rev. T. S. Mills,) meet alternately here and at Upper Mill.

A fair was first established at Dobcross on the last Thursday in July, 1828, and a second fair is intended to be held at this place on the second Thursday in March, 1829. These two fairs are to be held annually, for the sale of horned cattle, horses, pigs, and pedlary.

In the valley below Dobcross, lies Tame Water, the very elegant mansion of the Harrops, in the front of which is a fine display of horticultural neatness, much heightened in regard of the scenery, by the meanderings of the Tame amidst a luxuriance of meadow land, gracefully divided by neat cut edge rows, and terminated by a substantial bridge over the stream before mentioned.

> " Oh let me in this valley range,
> 'Tis here I breathe, 'tis here I live!
> Lo the grand scene of aged mountains,
> Smiling vallies, murm'ring fountains;
> Lambs in flow'ry pastures bleating,
> *Echo* our complaints repeating;
> Bees with busy sounds delighting,
> Groves to gentle sleep inviting.

Whispering winds the poplars courting,
Nymphs and Swains in circles sporting;
Birds in cheerful notes expressing,
Nature's bounty and their blessing:
These afford a lasting pleasure,
Without guilt and without measure."

Altered from Brown.

Above Tame Water stands the *Parsonage,* the present residence of the Rev. T. S. Mills, commanding an agreeable prospect of the village of Dobcross, and the surrounding hills.

A short distance from hence is situate a small place called *Husteads,* on the banks of a swift gliding stream, which soon after discharges its waters into the Tame, below the place named Tame Water.

On the road betwixt Dobcross and Delph, are a few ancient cottages called *Platt Lane,* from which place you have a fine prospect of the extensive valley beneath and of all the surrounding hills, as far as Friar's Mere, north, and Aldermans, south.

This part finishes our first tour in this romantic valley, only we have to remark that *Freeze Land,* so called, did not exactly come within our notice, lying wide of the main road. It is a district of scattered stone built, and chiefly ancient habitations, lying on the sides of the cheerless ridge of Alphin, of whom Bottomley writes

"O'er ALPHIN'S top, each morning from the main,
The sun twice rises on the adjacent plain,

Yet thrice the moon her revolution makes,
While Sol's bright beam the northern front forsakes,
Fix'd in the shade, as long fair *Freezland* mourns,
'Till from the south great Phœbus back returns;
Then with new charms his absence he repays,
With blooming fields, and groves, and length of days."

Our next tour commences by entering the district of Saddleworth at *Hey Chapel*, a village partly in the parish of Ashton-under-Lyne, and partly in Saddleworth; it contains a chapel of the establishment, dedicated to St. John. It is a substantial building of stone, erected in 1742, and consecrated June 26th, 1744; there is a cemetery adjoining, surrounded with a stone wall; a new cemetery however has lately been consecrated, on Wednesday, December 10th, 1828, by Dr. J. B. Sumner, the present bishop of Chester; this lies a short distance from the chapel, on the road to Lees, and in the hamlet of Lees. The chapel has been considerably enlarged since its first erection. It contains an organ, and formerly had a good attendance of both vocal and instrumental performers. It was here the celebrated Mrs. Bates first displayed her vocal powers, her brother being organist.

The first minister was the Rev. Richard Hopwood, of Oldham. After Mr. Hopwood, succeeded the Rev. John Becket, who was born at Wray, a village near Lancaster, on Holy Thursday, 1742. In 1761, he was elected master of the Free Grammar School of his own village, and in 1764 ordained Deacon, by bishop

Keene. He was curate of Saddleworth about two years, and incumbent minister of Lees, or Hey Chapel, near forty five years. He died universally regretted, October 24th, 1810, in the 69th year of his age. The present worthy incumbent is the Rev. William Winter, who is also incumbent of St. Peter's, Oldham, his assistant curate is the Rev. — Mattison.

In and near Hey chapel are several large cotton manufactories, and some respectable shops, with two public houses, the oldest of which has been kept for a long time by Mrs. Wrigley, who is of the family of the Houghtons, who have long resided here. They are a collateral branch of the family of the Houghtons, of Houghton Tower. Though the chapel of Hey, or Lees, is subject to and in the gift of the Rector of Ashton-under-Lyne, yet it lies on the extreme boundary and a great part of the village is in the Chapelry of Saddleworth.

On a steep hill above Hey Chapel stands the village of *Austerlands*, commanding a very extensive prospect over the circumjacent country. Here is a large cotton manufactory, and a very considerable number of well built cottages.

The turnpike road from Oldham to Huddersfield also passes through the place, from the former of which it is distant about two and a half miles east, and fourteen and a half from the latter, W. N. W.

The very large village of Waterhead Mill, is now extending fast up the hill into the Chapelry of Saddleworth, and if trade continues is likely to connect itself therewith in a series of years. In the valley beneath Austerlands is the detached hamlet of *Shelderslow*, consisting of several ancient dwellings, chiefly occupied by families employed in the surrounding cotton mills.

Near Shelderslow is *Claytons*, an ancient mansion, formerly occupied by a family of the local name. The initials of " I. A. C. A. C. 1659," are still remaining upon the building.

Ascending the eminences above, and again descending, on the left of *Black Leach*, at about half a mile distant from Shelderslow, we reach *Wood Brook*, a small village a short distance to the south of the Huddersfield Road, and on the banks of a branch of the Medlock, and about two miles west of Dobcross; again ascending the elevation above, we come to Scout Head, an ancient residence, adjoining which and in front of the road is a large cotton mill, with a neat modern mansion near it. A short distance hence, but nearer Austerlands is a well known Inn, called the *Three Crowns*, and some dwellings connected thereto.

Pursuing our journey towards New Delph, on the left appears the wild and bleak ridge of high land, denominated *High Moor*, on which are scattered a considerable number of detached dwellings, and upon this place named High Moor are several quarries of excellent stone, much used of late by the Manchester and other builders.

Leaving Scout Head, and journeying on the said road towards Huddersfield, we reach *New Houses*, a small hamlet, situated at the junction of a road from Lydgate, with the aforesaid one, being about one and a half miles from Dobcross; from hence an extended prospect opens on the eye of the spectator, the great expanded valley of Saddleworth presents itself, crowned by the heights of Standedge and Pule, and all the dreary moorlands in their vicinity; the church of Saddleworth, and the villages around are also visible.

Descending from these heights, we arrive at *Wall Hill*, a compactly built cluster of habitations, about one mile west of Dobcross. Wall Hill derives its name from the springs for which it is celebrated.

By a gradual slope downwards, we arrive at *Albion Cottage*, a small but genteel habitation, near *Thurston Clough*,* which is a romantic ravine, through which a branch of the Tame rushes down to join the parent stream; here are several cottages, and a public house; the descent again is almost gradual, till we come to *Stones*, a truly pleasing retreat, lying immediately under a high and rocky hill of the same name. The surrounding foliage of the varied plantations, and the fine lawn sloping to the road from the house, cause it to appear as one of the most striking objects in the valley, the house too being also rough cast, is thus rendered still more conspicuous; the Tame is seen herefrom, gliding along the richly cultivated valley below.

> "With woods o'erhung, and shagg'd with mossy rocks,
> Whence wildly down the gushing waters play,
> And then in bright meanders Tame is seen,
> Gleaming in lengthened vista thro' the trees,
> Here let me steal, and sit within the shade
> Of vernal trees, that tuft the swelling mounts,

* Perhaps from Thor, and Stone, some Saxon Idol once worshipped here.

Thrown graceful round by Nature's careless hand,
Here pensive listen to the various voice
Of rural peace : the herds, the flocks, the birds,
The hollow whispering breeze, the plaint of rills,
That, purling down amid the twisted roots
Which creep around, their dewy murmurs shake
On the soothed ear."

Altered from Thomson.

A little below we reach the elegant village of *New Delph,* here is a well built stone bridge over the Tame, and several genteel and truly elegant mansions, to which are generally attached a beautiful lawn, or they are graced with small plantations, and beautiful patches of horticulture. Here also is a large and elegant Inn, for the accommodation of the coaches and other vehicles daily passing through this place, with numerous respectable travellers, who journey on this main road, from Manchester, (through Oldham) to Huddersfield; it being generally considered the half-way house between the said great commercial towns. New Delph is about one mile north of Dobcross, and half a mile from Delph, (now commonly called Old Delph) at New Delph, surrounded by shades, stands the very elegant mansion of J. Lees, Esq. named Delph Lodge. It is a beautiful stone fabric, which is further rendered more delightful by the shades aforesaid, and a graceful lawn in front.

A short distance to the east of New Delph, lie *Castle Shaw,* and *Castle Hill,* two small hamlets, rendered memorable as being the supposed Roman Castrum, which was evidently posited here, with a view to awe the surrounding country, and also undoubtedly as a resting place for the tired legions, in their march to *Cambodunum,* as has been before more fully remarked upon.

A short distance from Castleshaw is a quarry, where the stones are obtained on which the country people here bake their oaten cakes; this place is denominated *Bake Stone Delph.*

A little further we enter the large village of DELPH, (or *Delfe,* Saxon,) evidently derived from *Delwan,* Saxon, a mine or quarry, or large cavity formed by digging: it is situated in a considerable but narrow extent of valley. Delph forms a considerable street of stone habitations, and is situate on the road leading from Dobcross to the Junction, and thence to Rochdale,. from the first of which it is distant about one mile and a half, north east; from the second about two miles and three quarters, and from the last place about nine miles, south; it is also distant from Oldham about six miles. Here are several woollen manufactories, and a number of neat habitations. It is seated in a romontic situation on the Tame, where in rather a confined channel, its turbulent waters hurry along over shelving and projecting rocks, and the banks on each side are laid out in pleasant gardens and pasture grounds; a bridge of one arch is thrown over the stream, in the northern part of the village, connecting the more ancient part of Delph with that on the opposite bank. In this village are two Dissenting meeting houses, with Schools attached thereto.

The *Independent Chapel* is situated at the northern entrance thereinto from Junction, and is a substantial stone fabric, encircled by a burial ground, in which are the tombs of some of its departed members. It was originally erected in 1746, as appears from a stone over the door, in front of the building, though it has been rebuilt since that time. The interior is neatly pewed and contains a gallery. In this chapel is a brass plate, commemorative of the Rev. Thomas Gurnill, once minister of this chapel, who died March 6th, 1769, Æ. S. 34. Here is also a mural monument in memory of the late Rev. Noah Blackburn, pastor of this place, who died May 4th, 1821, aged 70. Also a tablet of white marble to the memory of Joseph, son of the late Rev. N. Blackburn, and three other brothers of the young man's. The present minister of this chapel is the Rev. John Holroyd.

The *Methodists' Chapel*, near the bridge, is a commodious place of worship, built of stone, and surrounded by a cemetery. To this latter place of worship belongs a spacious Sunday School, situate near the chapel, and which has an upper and lower room.

In the village is a receiving house for letters, and several Inns, the principal of which is the *Swan*, besides a very considerable number of respectable shops. Delph is situate not far from the centre of Saddleworth, being only a little to the north east of that precise point, and here the waters of the Tame are increased by the confluence of a mountain stream called *Hull Brook*.

On a very considerable elevation about a mile to the

north east of Delph, stands *Friar Mere Chapel,* of the establishment, a very remarkable object for many miles around ; it is situate on a bleak mountain, it is a plain and rather small fabric of stone, surmounted by a cupola, erected and consecrated by Bishop Keene, the then diocesan of Chester, in 1758 ; it was erected very probably, in consequence of the distance of the parochial chapel from this part of Saddleworth, being upwards of four miles. The present curate is the Rev. John Buckley, who resides in a neat mansion at the foot of the hill on which the chapel is erected, at a place called *Friar Lodge,* immediately below which stands the genteel residence of *Mr. Ainley,* Solicitor, surrounded by beautiful foliage.

On an eminence ascending almost perpendicularly from the Tame, and opposite to the village of Delph, is the hamlet of *Hill End,* in which is seen the very pleasant, rural, and picturesque mansion of J. Roberts, Junr. Esq. with a beautiful garden in front.

The road from Delph to Junction, runs along the side of a hilly ridge of land, commanding a pleasant view of the long extended vale, sloping down in continued irruguous and vernal banks, to the stream of the Tame, which flows along the whole extent of the valley.

> Here oft the milk-maid's ditty greets the ear,
> Resounding soft along the echoing vale ;
> Hark ! hark ! the notes all trembling, sweet and clear,
> Soft breaking on the incense-breathing gale.
> Here jocund youths their gambols oft renew,
> At morn, at noon, and eve they oft are seen ;
> Warm suns still tempt, and skies serene and blue,
> While Joy claps hands upon the cottage green.

At about three quarters of a mile distant from Delph, in a northerly direction, we come to the respectable and pleasant hamlet of *Linfits*, a few elegant mansions, one of which is the residence of J. Roberts, Senr. Esquire. The lands in this neighbourhood are chiefly divided (in a different manner to what they are in the greatest part of the chapelry,) by neat cut edge rows and small plantations.

About one mile more north easterly, lie the detached cluster of stone cottages called *New Tame*, being opposite to Old Tame, which is on the other side of the river. The valley below is secluded and romantic, and the drooping branches of the shades which impend over the Tame, display unique and beautiful scenery. The prospect from hence exhibits the hamlets of Junction, and also the venerable habitations which compose that of Denshaw, closed by the high arid and barren elevations, the cloud capped tops of which soar above the adjacent vallies.

Passing several small farms and lonely habitations, the detail of which it would be tedious to particularize, one of which lies rather secluded from the rest, and is named *Broad Meadow*, the residence of the Shaws, we now arrive at *Denshaw*, from *Den*, Saxon, a cave, cavern, or hollow, and *Shaw*, Belgic, a thicket or small wood. It is a small village situate on the side of a hill, detached and scattered on the road from Junction to Huddersfield; the Tame below this place flows rapidly along, over flat shelving rocks, giving a romantic air and effect to the scenery around.

An ancient house in this village has these initials

over a door attached thereto, "I. C. E. 1666," which I remarked more particularly as being the year of the great fire in London.

A little nearer Junction, is a small building used as a Sunday School, which was erected in 1824, by subscription, promoted amongst the inhabitants of the surrounding country. Messrs. Buckley, Roberts & Co. bankers, of Saddleworth, gave the land whereon it is erected. The following Latin inscription is on a stone on the front thereof:

" Eruditio utilis moribus urbanis."

The *Junction*, is on the whole an elegant hamlet; here is a large, commodious, and genteel Inn, denominated from the meeting of the roads, *Junction Inn;* the roads from Oldham and Manchester, the road from Rochdale, that from Halifax, that from Huddersfield, and that from Delph, Dobcross, &c. all connect with each other here, and the Inn aforesaid, and the hamlet bears the name of Junction.

The barren moors above on the roads leading towards Halifax, and Huddersfield, form a proper contrast to the more fertile lands in the valley beneath. They are much frequented by the lovers of game, which abound in great plenty here.

"The murd'rous gun,
Glanc'd just and sudden, from the fowler's eye,
O'ertakes their sounding pinions, and again,
Immediate brings them from the tow'ring wing,
Dead to the ground; or drives them wide dispers'd,
Wounded, and wheeling various, down the wind."
Thomson.

And the lovers of the chase have here full scope to pursue their diversions, without the interpositions of walls and hedges, but

> " Poor is the triumph o'er the timid hare!
> Scar'd from the corn, and now to some lone seat
> Retir'd; the rushy fen, the ragged furze;
> Stretch'd o'er the stony heath, the stubble chapt;
> The thistly lawn, the thick-entangled broom;
> Of the same friendly hue the wither'd fern;
> The fallow ground laid open to the sun,
> Concoctive; and the nodding sandy bank,
> Hung o'er the mazes of the mountain brook:
> Vain is her best precaution, tho' she sits
> Conceal'd, with folded ears, unsleeping eyes,
> By Nature rais'd to take th' horizon in,
> And head couch'd close betwixt her hairy feet,
> In act to spring away. The scented dew
> Betrays her early labyrinth! and deep,
> In scatter'd sullen openings, far behind,
> With every breeze she hears the coming storm:
> But nearer, and more frequent, as it loads
> The sighing gale, she springs amaz'd, and all
> The savage soul of game is up at once:
> The pack full-opening, various; the shrill horn
> Resounding from the hills; the neighing steed,
> Wild for the chase; and the loud hunter's shout;
> O'er a weak, harmless, flying creature, all
> Mix'd in mad tumult and discordant joy.
>
> These are not subjects for the peaceful muse,
> Nor will she stain with such her spotless song,
> Then most delighted when she social sees
> The whole mix'd animal creation round
> Alive and happy."   *Ibid.*

In a solitary part of the country, to the north of the Junction aforesaid, lies a small place denominated *Cherry Clough*, bordering upon the dreary wilds of the township of Crompton, in the Parochial Chapelry of Oldham; near which also lies *Cherry Clough Yate*, a similar place.

Leaving Cherry Clough, and ascending to some heights called *Saddleworth Wall*, being the division line of the two districts or chapelries of Saddleworth and Oldham, we descend to *Wood Brow*, the mansion of Thomas Gartside, Esq. a stone edifice, with a neat parterre in front. The brown and barren heath above, with the great capacious valley of Friar Mere in the fore ground, and the long chain of hills on each side, form from hence a fine and striking prospect. The Oldham and Halifax road runs just below, and on the line of it, a little above is *Calf Hey*, a small irregularly built place; nearly adjoining which is *Old Tame*, a similar small hamlet, in which are two respectable public houses, for the accommodation of the numerous travellers, passing and repassing to and from the two adjoining counties of York and Lancaster. Old Tame is about two and a half miles N. E. from Delph, near which is situate a small hamlet, called *Hollin Bank*, and still further a place called *Street Cut*, which lies a little below *Grains*, this is a small village, a part of which is in Oldham and the other in Saddleworth; it consists of a number of dwellings, situated on a bleak eminence, overlooking the very extensive valley between the village of Delph and the Junction.

Along the sides of the hills from Grains to Delph, is

an irregular road of about three miles in length; here are two public houses. Grains is the most north westerly part of Saddleworth, though by no means an inviting portion of this district.

The following small hamlets lying out of the regular line of our tours through the chapelry, I venture to remark upon at the close of this account, viz. *Bottoms*, which is a small hamlet with a cotton spinning concern, and distant from Dobcross about two miles.

Causeway Sett is a very small hamlet, about the same distance from Dobcross.

Clough Bottom, a similar place, at a like distance from the said village.

Doctor Houses is a small manufacturing hamlet, one mile from Dobcross, near which is *Doctor Lane Head*.

Fair Banks, a hamlet two miles and a quarter from the aforesaid place; also *Grange*, a collection of about seven or eight habitations, a short distance from Delph.

Lane Head, a hamlet chiefly inhabited by woollen manufacturers, situate at the distance of about two miles from Dobcross, with *Manns*, a small place at an equal distance from the aforesaid.

Old Hey, consists of three or four houses, in the vicinity of Delph.

Pob Green, at the distance of nearly two miles from Dobcross.

Primrose, a small place inhabited by the manufacturers of Saddleworth goods, distant two miles and a quarter from the last mentioned village.

Roe Buck Loe, on an eminence, as the name imports

where the *deer stood at bay*, when this part of the country exhibited one dreary wilderness or forest; this consists of a small hamlet of houses, situate about one mile and a half from **Dobcross.**

Sand Bed, consisting of only three or four houses, is in the neighbourhood of the said before mentioned village. *Shaws*, also a small hamlet, at the distance of one mile and a half from Dobcross aforesaid, with *Slades Barn*, which is also a small place, situate about one mile and a quarter from the village before named.

Top o'th' Meadow is within this chapelry; here is both a cotton and coal concern, and lies at the distance of about three miles from Oldham; there is also a small hamlet named *Wellyhole*, near to the village of Mossley, being distant therefrom about one mile.

White Lee has passed as yet unnoticed, being a straggling hamlet near *Lane Head*, in Saddleworth.

Strines, and *Strines Dale*, with *Pastures*, in the vicinity of Waterhead Mill, through which flows a branch of the Medlock, separating the two parochial chapelries of Oldham and Saddleworth, and also the counties of Lancaster and York.

Waterhead Mill, from a small place consisting of a few cottages, about thirty years ago, called *Mill Bottom*, has risen into eminence, and may now be considered as one of the first leading villages of this country, the cotton manufactories built here, and employing hundreds of its population, has induced the owners of the same, and other persons to erect cottages, for the convenience of the mechanics, and those other labourers employed in these works, and by this means it has branched out in every direction, both on the road to Oldham, and on that to Saddleworth, and also on the ascent of the hill, in the direction of Podem, within the Chapelry of Oldham, in which chapelry the greatest part of the village of Waterhead Mill is situated, and the rest in Saddleworth, on the road to Austerlands. In the village are a number of respectable shops, and six public houses, the principal one of which is the *Coach and Horses*. We omitted to observe that there is a Day and Sunday School established, on the very summit of the hill called Warmton.

On the moorlands of Saddleworth is found (though but seldom,) a particular species of plant, which Mr. Gough says some of our naturalists call in Latin, *Vaccinia Nubis*, but the more common and true name is *Rubis Chamæmorus*, or in English, Cloudsberry, as if produced (says Camden,) by the clouds. It is a kind of dwarf mulberry, and though *Camden* observes " it is peculiar only to Pendle Hill, in Lancashire," he must be much mistaken, as it is found both in Yorkshire and Cheshire, on the moorlands of both those two counties, and plentifully on most of the boggy tops of the high mountains in England and Scotland. In Norway also and the other northern regions it is abundantly found. Cranberries however are more plentifully found in the Saddleworth hills than the former, the Latin name of which is *Vaccinium Oxycoccus*. Whinberries or Bilberries are however the most common berry, and quite plentiful, and employ a vast number of young people in the summer months, in picking them.

In the morasses or mosses, whence the country people dig their turf, or peat, for the use of fuel, there have been often found marine shells, a few cones, nuts and shells, trunks of fir trees, and fir apples, with many other exotic substances. The morasses in which these substances are found, are frequently upon the summit of high mountains; the learned have been greatly divided in their opinions upon or how they came there. The general opinion however is that they were brought there by the Deluge, not merely from their situation, but because seven or eight trees are frequently found much closer to each other than it was possible for them to grow, and under these trees are frequently found the exuviæ of animals, as shells, and bones of fishes, and particularly the head of a hippopotamus was dug up in one of the moors of the adjoining county of Chester, and shewn to Dr. Leigh, the author of the natural history of Cheshire.

There are however substances found of a much later date than our chronologists fix the time of the General Deluge, among these trees and exuviæ, particularly a brass kettle, a small stone, and amber beads, which were given to the aforesaid author. The fir trees have been dug up here, and in many other places than the moorlands of Saddleworth, and contain so much turpentine, that splinters of them have been often substituted by the country peasants in lieu of candles.

Moorlands which are in a state of nature and produce heath, and other wild plants, are of various qualities and different natures, being very extensive in the neighbourhood of this chapelry, and much more so than might have been expected, in a country now so populous as Saddleworth, and consequently where land must be so much wanted, and therefore become so valuable.

The mosses, or morasses, are large tracts of land, which by their brown and barren appearance greatly deform the face of the country. They consist of a spongy soil, composed of the roots of decayed vegetables, in different states of decomposition. The surface of these mosses is turfy, and below is a black, moist, and spongy earth, which being dug up with spades, and almost cut out in the form of bricks, and laid in pyramidal heaps to dry, is what they call peat, and is used in Saddleworth, (where coals are scarce) and other places as fuel, and they sometimes contain so much bituminous matter as to burn with a flame; the trees found herein, (as before stated,) are discovered generally buried several feet below the surface of these morasses, and so well preserved by the exclusion of air, that they are capable of being wrought into furniture. After penetrating through the moss earth, or bed of peat, a strata of sand or clay is often found, so that it is very evident these tracts were once forest land, the trees upon which were destroyed by an inundation of salt water.

The Tame river which falls into the Mersey, (says an author) is remarkable for eels, which are so fat that few people can eat them; the fatness of which (says he) is attributable to the grease and oil with which it is impregnated, exuding from the number of goods passing through the woollen mills erected on its banks.

"The Saddleworth people, (says Baines) like the mountaineers of Switzerland, have a character peculiar to themselves: They are rude of speech," (perhaps more honest in their motives than their politer and more polished neighbours, he might have added, for I am tempted to think we generally find it so,) "but" (they are, adds he) "kind and hospitable in disposition, without many of the benefits of education," (here Mr. Baines and me again run counter in opinion, for I find them more generally enlightened than in some parishes nearer Manchester,) "but of quick perception, and sound judgment. They mix little in the world," (query, is this correct?) " their own deep vallies, and lofty mountains form a world of their own, in which as much comfort and solid contentment exist, as fall to the lot of the generality of mankind." Now the natives of this valley I generally find, possess more enlightened notions of polity, more liberality of principle, more independence of spirit, joined to less enthusiastic notions in religious matters, (now so generally prevalent, in the neighbouring parishes,) with all that quick preception, soundness of judgment, and honesty of intention, so indispensible to the formation of a character, deserving of our esteem, admiration, and imitation. This of the men; the female part, joined to all that softness, kindness, and affability of the sex, (the lower orders or working classes here) possess a peculiar modesty of manner not to be found in more populous places; this may be attributable in some degree perhaps, to their not so frequently meeting together as in large towns, at the chit chat (not to say scandal and immoral) parties of the tea table, but also their greater seclusion from those too generally scenes of vice and immorality, (I wish I could with truth use a softer term,) which but too often disgrace the very large mills and manufactories, particularly in the cotton trade.

    Reluctant now, thy vale belov'd, recedes from view,
    And to thy nymphs, and mountaineers, I bid adieu.

ADDENDA
TO
SADDLEWORTH.

In page 7, copied from some remarks by Mr. Bottomley, a correspondent observes, that "in the steep part where horses cannot be used, the land is seldom or scarcely ever ploughed for corn." However I am inclined to think this was customary at the time Mr. B. wrote the remarks I quoted.

In page 9, line 8th, it is stated that Lord's Mere lies to the west, for which read *south east*, and Shaw Mere to the *south east*, for which read *betwixt Lord's Mere and Quick Mere.*

In 1782, the population of Saddleworth was 6918, and the number of horses then kept was 416.

In page 13, line 12, for 1065, read 10,065, and same page, line 13, for 1321, read 1821.

In page 27, line 11, for Goldwick, read *Glodwick.*

In page 26, line 11, after the word "*Modistus*" read "*the victorious Centurion of the sixth pious and faithful Legion.*" This is the correct translation.

Page 55, line 26, for Boarshaw, read *Boarshurst.*

Page 61, line 17, for worm, read *reptile worm.*

INDEX

TO THE
HISTORY OF SADDLEWORTH.

	Page.		Page.
Altar, Roman	25	Cross	57
Ancient account of Friar Mere	29	Cross Keys	58
		Court	58
Annexation to Rochdale	36	Claytons	66
Aldermans, hill of 22.	52	Castle Hill	68
Agriculture	6	Cherry Clough	75
Air	8	Cherry Clough Yate	75
Ancient state	16	Calf Hey	75
Antiquities, Druidical	17	Curious Discoveries 78	79
Alphin, hill of 51	63	Description of Saddleworth	5
Austerlands	65	Divisions	9
Albion Cottage	67	Druidical Remains	17
British Words	16	Druidical Antiquities	19
Bells	39	Druids, customs of the	23
Brookbottom	47	Diggle, observations on the word	16
Boarshurst	50		
Bills o' Jacks	53	Diggle, rivulet 9	58
Black Hey Nook	59	Diggle, Bridge	58
Brown Hill	60	Danes, supposed march of the	28
Black Leach	66		
Bake Stone Delph	69	Dove Stones	52
Broad Meadow	72	Dobcross, village of	60
Canal, the Huddersfield	10	Dobcross Chapel	66
Customs of the Druids	23	Dobcross Free School	61
Castleshaw 68	24	Delph, New	68
Course of the Roman roads 27	37	Delph, village of	69
		Delph, Bake Stone	69
Charters, ancient	33	Doctor Houses	76
Curious relic	39	Doctor Lane Head	76
Curious epitaphs 40	41	Denshaw	72
Carr	59	Discoveries, Curious 78	79
Carr Hill	47	Employment	13

INDEX

	Page		Page
Etymology of Saddleworth	15	Hollin Bank	75
Essay on Druidical remains	17	Interior of the Church	37
Enlargement of the Church	38	Incumbents of Saddleworth	36
Epitaphs, curious	40, 41	Incumbent's Salary	41
Friar Mere, ancient account of	29	Inhabitants of Saddleworth	81
Foundation of the Church	33	Independent Chapel, Delph	70
Foul Rakes	50	Junction, Junction Inn	73
Fairy Holes, account of the	53	Junction School	73
Far Lane	57	Lane Head	76
Fearn Lee	58	Lees, village of	45
Freeze Land	63	Lydgate	46
Friar Mere Chapel	71	Lydgate, Chapel of	46
Friar Lodge	71	Linfits	72
Fair Banks	76	List, topographical, of hamlets, &c.	76
General description of Saddleworth	5	Manufactures of Saddleworth	13
Grotton Head	47	Manns	76
Grove	48	March of the Danes	28
Grass Croft, village of	48	Mossley Hall	47
Grasscroft Clough	48	Marslands	59
Green Bridge	50	Moorlands, observations on	78
Greenfield, valley of	49	New Houses	66
Greenfield, romantic beauties of	51	New Delph	68
		New Tame	72
Greenfield Mill	51	Organ of the Church	39
Grains	75	Oak view	50
General remarks on Saddleworth	82	Old Tame	75
		Observations on the Moorlands	78
Grange	76	Parochial Chapelry of Saddleworth	5
Hills	8		
Huddersfield Canal, the	10		
Holly Ville	50	Parochial Chapel, account of the	31
Heath Fields	57	Population	13
Hollin Greave	58	Pots and Pans, remarks on	17
Hollins	58	Proprietors of the soil	29
Harrop Edge	58	Parsonage, state of the	34
Husteads	63	Parsonage, Dobcross	62
Hey, village of	64	Privileges of the Church	41
Hey, Chapel of	65	Platt Lane	63
Hey, Old	76	Pob Green	76
High Moor	66	Primrose	76
Hill End	71		

INDEX

	Page		Page
Pastures	77	Stone Breaks	45
Prospects 37, 46, 47, 48, 48, 50, 51, 52, 57, 58, 62, 63, 66, 67, 71, 72, 75		Shaw Hall	48
		Standedge	58
		Sheldersloe	66
Quick	47	Stones	67
Quick Edge	47	Saddleworth Wall	75
Rivers, Chaw, Tame, Diggle	9	Street Cut	75
Roads, ancient and modern	11	Topographical description	43
Romans, the	24	Thornley, or Thornlee	46
Roman's Castleshaw	24	Tunstead	57
Roman Roads 27	37	Tame, river 9, 16,	80
Roman Altar	25	Tame Water	62
Ravenstones	52	Thurston Clough	67
Running Hill Head	59	Topographical list of hamlets	76
Roebuck Loe	76		
Romantic beauties, 48, 50, 52, 53, 58, 59, 60, 62, 67, 69, 71, 72.		Upper Mill, village of	43
		Upper Mill, Dissenters Chapels	44
Saddleworth, Parochial Chapelry of	5	Vallies	8
		Villages, Hamlets, &c.	13
Saddleworth, Parochial Chapel of	31	Ville, Holly	50
		Watson's Account of Castleshaw	24
Saddleworth, etymology of	15	Walkers	45
Saddleworth, inhabitants of	81	Warmton	48
Saddleworth, Curates of	36	Warwick Hill and Foot	58
Saddleworth, moorlands of	78	Workhouse	59
Saddleworth Fold	57	Weaky	59
Springs, Streams	9	Wool Road	60
Stapletons 29,	33	Wood Brook	66
Stapeley Stones	21	Wall Hill	67
Situation of the Church	37	Wood Brow	75
Sunday Schools	42	Waterhead Mill	77
Spring Head	45		

Printed by W. D. VAREY, Manchester.